FAMILY GUIDE

Dan and Joy Solomon
Creators

Debra Ball-Kilbourne
MaryJane Pierce Norton
Writers

FAITHHOME FAMILY GUIDE

Copyright © 1997 by Abingdon Press

CIP data available from the Library of Congress
ISBN 0-687-06590-9

This book is printed on recycled, acid-free paper.

Scripture quotations are from the New Revised Standard
Version Bible. Copyright © 1989 by the Division of Christian
Education of the National Council of the Churches of Christ
in the United States of America. Used by permission.

97 98 99 00 01 02 03 04 05 06 — 10 9 8 7 6 5 4 3 2 1

MANUFACTURED IN THE UNITED STATES OF AMERICA

Contents

Introduction 5

Week 1
Day 1: Getting Started 11
Day 2: New Habits 13
Day 3: New Learnings 16
Day 4: Talking About God: In the Beginning 18
Day 5: Talking About God: Maker of Heaven and Earth 22
Day 6: Talking About God: Honored by Many Names 24
Day 7: Talking About God: God the Father 27
Family Meals 29
Reaching Beyond the Family 31

Week 2
Day 1: Talking About God: New Sharings 32
Day 2: Talking About God: God the Creator 34
Day 3: Talking About God: It Was Good 36
Day 4: Talking About Jesus: The Core of Christianity 39
Day 5: Talking About Jesus: Completely God 43
Day 6: Talking About Jesus: Completely Human 44
Day 7: Talking About Jesus: God's Only Son, Our Lord 46
Family Meals 48
Reaching Beyond the Family 51

Week 3
Day 1: Talking About Jesus: New Sharings 52
Day 2: Talking About Jesus: Suffered, Crucified, Buried 54
Day 3: Talking About Jesus: He Rose from the Dead 58
Day 4: Talking About the Holy Spirit: Pentecost 60
Day 5: Talking About the Holy Spirit: Wind 63
Day 6: Talking About the Holy Spirit: Fire 66
Day 7: Talking About the Holy Spirit: New Birth 68
Family Meals 71
Reaching Beyond the Family 74

Week 4
Day 1: Talking About the Holy Spirit: New Sharings 75
Day 2: Talking About the Holy Spirit: Waiting for the Spirit 77
Day 3: Talking About the Holy Spirit: One in Three Persons 79
Day 4: We Are a Learning Church: Teach Them to Your Children 83
Day 5: We Are a Learning Church: Learning to Do Good 87
Day 6: We Are a Learning Church: Learning the Rules 89
Day 7: We Are a Learning Church: Not Everyone Has to Do Things the Same . . 91
Family Meals 94
Reaching Beyond the Family 96

Week 5

Day 1: We Are a Learning Church: Obedience 97
Day 2: We Are a Learning Church: Lifelong Learning 99
Day 3: We Are a Learning Church: Learning to Love and Respect God 102
Day 4: We Are a Worshiping Church: Sunday 104
Day 5: We Are a Worshiping Church: Praise 108
Day 6: We Are a Worshiping Church: Movement 110
Day 7: We Are a Worshiping Church: Sermon 113
Family Meals. 115
Reaching Beyond the Family 117

Week 6

Day 1: We Are a Worshiping Church: The Ritual of Baptism 118
Day 2: We Are a Worshiping Church: The Ritual of Holy Communion 120
Day 3: We Are a Worshiping Church: Offering 123
Day 4: We Are a Witnessing and Serving Church: Don't Hide Your Light ... 125
Day 5: We Are a Witnessing and Serving Church: Sharing with Other
    Christians 129
Day 6: We Are a Witnessing and Serving Church: Sharing with Others Who
    Are Not Like Us 131
Day 7: We Are a Witnessing and Serving Church: Justice 134
Family Meals. 136
Reaching Beyond the Family 138

Week 7

Day 1: We Are a Witnessing and Serving Church: Peace 139
Day 2: We Are a Witnessing and Serving Church: Charity (Love) 141
Day 3: We Are a Witnessing and Serving Church: Hospitality 144
Day 4: Living with the Bible: Scripture. 146
Day 5: Living with the Bible: In Order That You Might Believe 150
Day 6: Living with the Bible: Helping to Understand 152
Day 7: Living with the Bible: Sweeter Than Honey 154
Family Meals. 156
Reaching Beyond the Family 158

Week 8

Day 1: Living with the Bible: Scripture Fulfilled 159
Day 2: Living with the Bible: A Daily Habit 161
Day 3: Living with the Bible: More Than Study. 163
Day 4: Living Sacramentally: Recognizing God's Presence Every Day 166
Day 5: Living Sacramentally: Family Rituals. 170
Day 6: Living Sacramentally: Daily Bread/Daily Prayer 173
Day 7: Living Sacramentally: Pray Without Ceasing 175
Family Meals. 177
Reaching Beyond the Family 179

Week 9

Day 1: Living Sacramentally: Humble Service 180
Day 2: Living Sacramentally: Continuing. 182
Day 3: Living Sacramentally: With You Always. 184
Family Meals. 186
Reaching Beyond the Family 188

Recommended Resources 189

Endnotes 192

Introduction

Welcome to FaithHome, an exciting and fun experience in which you and your family will join other families in learning about God, the Christian faith, and how to be a "faith home"—a home in which talking about God and talking to God are a natural and comfortable part of your everyday family life. Through the FaithHome experience, your family also will discover that you are an important part of a larger "faith home," the church, where you both receive and give love, guidance, support, security, and encouragement as you seek to be faithful families in today's world.

During your FaithHome experience, you and your family will explore basic beliefs about

- God
- Jesus
- the Holy Spirit
- prayer
- the church
- worship
- baptism and Holy Communion
- serving others
- and other basic beliefs of the Christian faith

As you spend time discussing these topics—so vital to developing your children's faith foundation—it is our hope that you will forge new bonds within your own family and with other Christian families who are experiencing FaithHome with you.

HOW DOES FAITHHOME WORK?

Over the next nine weeks, your family will take part in a weekly session in the church building that focuses on the topics listed above. Each session will last approximately 75-90 minutes. During the session you will view a short video segment; participate with other families in fun activities, discussions, singing, and worship; and break into separate groups of adults and children for a time of focused learning and sharing. After the weekly group experience, you are to continue learning and sharing together as a family during the following week, using this *Family Guide*. The ideas and suggestions provided here will help you to develop, practice, and continue important habits—such as regular family prayers, meals, devotions, faith conversations, and outreach activities—that will draw you closer together and closer to God as you make a serious commitment to make your home a "faith home."

In addition to learning and understanding the Apostles' Creed, one of the earliest statements of belief of the Christian faith, your family will also be learning the Lord's Prayer. Perhaps you will want to begin or end the day by saying this prayer together. Another way to make the prayer of our Savior more familiar could be to pray it together each day just before or after the prayer during your "Family Faith Break" time.

HOW DO I USE THIS FAMILY GUIDE?

Your *Family Guide* has been designed to be convenient and easy to use. Throughout its pages you will find the following helpful sections:

 BACKGROUND BASICS

Here you will find background material related to the beliefs and ideas you will be exploring together in your weekly FaithHome gathering at the church. Some of the material may be familiar to you; some will be new to you. In either case, you will find it helpful to review this material prior to your weekly FaithHome group experience. Before attending your first FaithHome gathering, you will read the "Background Basics" provided at the beginning of Week 1. Then, for the first three days following the gathering, you will continue to explore that topic in conversations and devotions with your family at home. The material provided in your *Family Guide* for Days 4–7 will begin to acquaint your family with the topic for the second FaithHome gathering. You will find the "Background Basics" for the second FaithHome gathering with the material provided for Day 4. Likewise, each week you will be reading "Background Basics" related to the upcoming FaithHome gathering on Day 4.

 TAKE NOTE

This icon indicates a helpful explanation or suggestion, a related insight, or an idea for further reflection. The information found here is not "extra" but essential for a successful and rewarding FaithHome experience.

 TOGETHER

Each day you will find a section headed "Talk Together." You should do exactly that: Talk together! The time you choose to do this is up to you. Perhaps you eat breakfast together each morning and can use the "Talk Together" suggestions then—or during another family meal. Or you might talk for a few minutes in the evening before a television show that the whole family enjoys watching together, or before bedtime. You might even talk about some of the ideas while riding in the car on the way to school, to church, or to other activities. If time permits, you might want to begin your daily "Family Faith Break" (see below) with the "Talk Together" suggestions for that day. The important thing is that you find time to talk together as a family each day. Talking together will help you to grow as a family and as individuals.

For the first three days of each week, your conversations will focus on themes related to the weekly FaithHome gathering you have just experienced. For the last four days of each week, your conversations will focus on themes related to the next weekly gathering.

 ## FAMILY FAITH BREAK

Every day during your FaithHome experience, you will be expected to take a few minutes for a "Family Faith Break." Unlike the "Talk Together" suggestions, which may be used throughout the day whenever you can find time to talk as a family, your "Family Faith Break" should be a planned, more structured time of sharing. Each of these breaks will include the following:

- reading aloud from the Bible
- time for reflection, usually involving the Bible passage read aloud
- guided discussion and sharing
- prayer time together

As with the "Talk Together" suggestions, the "Family Faith Breaks" for the first three days of each week will focus on themes related to the weekly FaithHome gathering you have just experienced; those for the last four days of the week will focus on themes related to the next weekly gathering.

These "Family Faith Breaks" should last no more than ten to fifteen minutes. Attempt to make them quality time experiences. How can you do that? Here are a few suggestions:

- As much as possible, hold your "Family Faith Breaks" at times when all family members are available.
- Turn off the television, radio, and CD player.
- Ignore the telephone for a few minutes.
- Choose a time and place for your "Family Faith Breaks" that will allow all family members to pay attention to one another, to the words of the Bible, to the ideas and questions being shared, and to God.
- As often as possible, hold your "Family Faith Breaks" at the same

time each day. For example, gather for a few minutes after or before a particular meal, or huddle together on someone's bed early in the morning or before bedtime. By doing this, even small children can begin to anticipate when the family will gather.

BIBLE HELP

Throughout this *Family Guide* you will find background information or helpful insights related to the biblical concepts and Scripture passages you will be exploring. This material is provided primarily for your own use so that you can help your family understand the passage or concept and its meaning for your lives. Share with your family as much of this information as you feel is appropriate or helpful.

FAMILY MEALS

With increasing demands on both parents and children, many families find it rare to eat together. Breakfast might be a toaster pastry on the fly; lunch might be whatever is offered in a work or school cafeteria; supper might be "out of the refrigerator" or fast food in the car, as children are transported to after-school activities. Yet mealtime is a wonderful time for families to do far more than just eat!

When your family eats together, you can share the events of the day—successes and failures. You can plan special events or outings. You can tell jokes and stories. Think of family meals as a time to

- share family stories, including stories about extended family and parents' childhoods;
- enjoy a more relaxed meal (With supper often "on the run," a more leisurely meal is enjoyed by everyone.);
- "check things out" with parents and siblings. Many important decisions are made and many hurts are healed around the family table.

At the end of the material provided for each week in this *Family Guide*, you will find plans for two family meals to be shared anytime during the week—whether it be breakfast, lunch, or supper. These "plans" include such things as menu ideas and recipes, suggestions for involving children in planning and preparation, table "rituals" (such as placing a Christ candle in the center of your table and lighting it for the meal), sample prayers, and conversation starters.

Though some menu ideas and recipes are provided, remember that the meals can be anything you like. Family meals do not require elaborate menus or the best china! In fact, one family says some of their best family meals have been pizza eaten on the deck. Those meals became memorable occasions because the family took time to enjoy both the pizza and one another! The important thing is to make the meal a special time for your family. As you continue this practice, you will discover that one of the best ways to grow closer together as a family is to express your love for one another and for God around the family table.

 ## REACHING BEYOND THE FAMILY

It is often said that experience is the best teacher. Perhaps there is no better way to help your children learn what it means to be a Christian than to put faith into action. As Christians, we are to reach beyond our own family members to serve the world.

Each week you will find a simple, practical idea for "reaching beyond the family" in love and service. While no idea will be a burden to your family, some will require more time and energy than others. Feel free to substitute another idea of your own creation for any suggestion offered in this book. The important thing is to do something each week to reach beyond your own family. As you do this, your family will grow in Christian love!

As you begin your FaithHome experience, remember that there are no perfect Christians and no perfect families. All of us continue to learn and grow as long as we live. Some of the things you will be doing together during the next nine weeks may be new to your family. Try to have realistic expectations of one another and, most important, to encourage and help one another as you and your family learn to be at home in the faith!

Day 1: Getting Started

Today you met for the first time with your FaithHome group and began an exciting journey that will help you and your family talk about what it means to be a Christian and what we believe as Christians. For the next few days you will talk more about what it means to live as Christians.

 ## BACKGROUND BASICS

In the early years of Christianity, a carefully crafted statement set forth beliefs that helped to shape Christian identity. Known today as the Apostles' Creed, the statement describes major Christian beliefs that Christians have sought to embody and live out in the world for two thousand years. They are essential beliefs for us to uphold and pass on to our children. For this reason, we will focus on the beliefs outlined in the Apostles' Creed throughout the FaithHome experience.

The apostles, or disciples of Jesus, might not have composed the creed themselves; they were dead long before the creed came into the written form we have today. They did, however, live out the message of the creed as followers of Jesus. Thus, the creed bears their name. The content of the creed was closely related to its use in baptismal services, perhaps as early as the first century following Jesus' ministry. Candidates for baptism were invited to declare their faith. To proclaim the creed was to embark on a new way of living—a lifestyle of apostleship.

As the Christian church has grown and spread throughout the world, Christians have affirmed their faith through many different creeds. Christians today not only affirm their faith through ancient creeds but also make fresh statements about God, Jesus, and the Holy Spirit. The Apostles' Creed, however, retains its importance as perhaps the earliest creed of the Christian movement. Its brevity, comprehensiveness, and bold witness make it a creed for followers of every age.

 ## TOGETHER

 ## TAKE NOTE

In order to make your "Talk Together" times successful, you will need to take responsibility for making sure quality communication takes place. Try these tips for talking together as a family:

- Encourage family members to share without fear of giving a wrong response. In FaithHome, no responses are "wrong" and no questions are "stupid."

- Do not put anyone on the spot. At any time, a family member may say "pass" and not have to share if he or she feels uncomfortable doing so.

- Be alert to any concerns that family members bring from "outside" the FaithHome experience. If appropriate, stop your FaithHome time to address an issue that is bothering a family member. When that issue has been dealt with so that everyone can focus again on FaithHome, resume your FaithHome discussion.

- Model good sharing. Be interested in what others say. Allow time— even silent time—for others to say something if they wish. Try not to be in a hurry to move along!

(1) As a family, try to remember as much as you can about your separate group experiences during the first FaithHome session and talk about them together.

(2) Invite each member of the family to share one thing that he or she heard during the session that was new or important to him or her.

 ## FAMILY FAITH BREAK

Your first "Family Faith Break" has five steps and concludes with prayer. Because your experience of reading the Bible, talking about it, and praying to God as a family may feel strange and even awkward at first, take your time. Have fun and help one another!

(1) Invite a member of your family to read aloud 1 Peter 2:9-10. Peter (or someone who may have learned about Jesus Christ from Peter's teachings) wrote this letter to new Christians in the region we now call Turkey. The Christians there struggled with some of the same questions and problems you and your family may struggle with, such as,

- Why are we Christians?
- What is important about being Christian?
- How is the way a Christian lives different from the way other people live?
- How might others around you who are not Christians act toward you?
- How should we live as a Christian family?

Some of the answers given in First Peter are limited by the differences in time, place, and culture between then and now. But many of the questions are indeed ones that we find ourselves struggling with today.

(2) As a family, select one of the questions listed on the preceding page that you consider especially important for your family. Why is this question important to your family?

(3) Read 1 Peter 2:9-10 aloud again. Then ask each family member to be quiet for a few moments and think about this Bible passage.

(4) Work together to put this passage into your own words—words that every family member can understand. Give each person a chance to say what the passage means to her or him.

(5) How may God be speaking to your family through this Bible passage, offering words that help you with the important question you have identified?

Prayer:

Ask if anyone has any hurts, needs, joys, or concerns to share aloud with the rest of the family. Explain what you mean by sharing some concerns of your own or by suggesting some that you have been aware of in the lives of other family members during the week. Even very young children can be encouraged to talk about things that have made them happy or sad during the week, such as playing outside or getting a skinned knee. Talk about how much God cares about us and what happens to us every day and about how God is always with us. God is always there, ready to listen to us and to help us in all that we do. We can talk to God just like we talk to a family member or a friend.

Say a short, simple prayer on behalf of the entire family, mentioning the specific needs, concerns, and joys named. Close with these words:

Dear God, we ask you to be with us and bless us as we take part in FaithHome. Help us to know in our hearts that we are your children, that you love us, and that you are always with us. We pray in Jesus' name. Amen.

Day 2: New Habits

What habits does your family have? Maybe your family . . .

- eats pizza every Friday night
- watches videos together on the weekend
- goes to church together
- tends to forget to give one another phone messages

- talks together about what has happened during the day
- has a bedtime routine
- prays together before meals

A habit is an ongoing pattern of behavior. Every family has patterns of behavior—or habits—just as every person does.

This FaithHome experience is intended, among other things, to help your family become more comfortable in the regular practice of Christian habits as a family—whether those habits be old or new to your family. Yesterday, for example, you began the practice of a daily "Family Faith Break," using the materials in this book as a guide. As you continue to do this, you will be acquiring the habits of reading and discussing the Bible together, praying together, and talking about God and faith. FaithHome also encourages you to develop the habit of sharing special family meals twice a week (see pages 29–31).

Some persons have observed that if a new pattern of behavior is practiced diligently for at least a month, it becomes a habit—an unconscious part of a person's ongoing behavior and character. FaithHome offers you two months' worth of family "guides" to help you form or strengthen these important Christian habits—habits that will

- help you as parents become more confident in your faith;
- build Christian character in your children (and in you!);
- help your family become familiar with what God has to say to you in the Bible;
- provide your family members with sound guidance for making lifestyle decisions;
- provide your children with experience in Christian practices and beliefs that will stay with them throughout their lives.

 ## TOGETHER

(1) Ask each family member to name at least one habit—whether good or bad—that your family has. Keep the focus on *family* habits, not on habits that individuals may have.

(2) Do these habits seem to be good habits or bad habits? Why?

(3) What makes a habit "good" or "bad"? (Encourage family members to explain their responses.)

(4) What makes a habit "Christian"? (Remember: There are no "wrong" or "stupid" answers. One example of a response to this question might be that a habit is "Christian" if it is something that Jesus might do. Other responses are possible and appropriate as well.)

FAMILY FAITH BREAK

(1) Ask a member of your family to read aloud Ephesians 4:22-24.

BIBLE HELP

Sometime in the late first century after Christ, either the apostle Paul or someone who had learned to be a Christian from Paul wrote to the Christians in Ephesus, a city on what is now the west coast of Turkey. The letter writer told the Ephesian Christians about what it meant for them to be Christians. The verses you are reading today are within a larger section contrasting the new way of life expected of the Ephesian Christians and their old way of living. In other words, being Christian means practicing different habits from those sometimes practiced by persons who are not Christian.

(2) If the children in your family are able to be patient while hearing or reading a longer passage from the Bible, have a family member read aloud Ephesians 4:17–5:20. If not, then read only 4:22-24 again. Ask each family member to listen for those things mentioned as old or "bad" habits and for those things mentioned as new or "good," Christian habits.

(3) Think of your life together as a family. What are some bad habits of your family that you would like to put behind you?

(4) What are some Christian habits that you already practice as a family?

(5) What are some new Christian habits your family might try to practice?

(6) Now read or reread Ephesians 5:8b-10: "Live as children of light—for the fruit of the light is found in all that is good and right and true. Try to find out what is pleasing to the Lord." Talk about what these verses mean and how the Christian habits you have talked about can help you live as children of light.

Prayer:

Build on yesterday's discussion of God's love and care for us and God's constant presence. Talk about how God can help us replace bad habits with good, Christian habits. When we ask God to help us, God responds like a loving, concerned parent. God hears our prayers and gives us what we need to live as Christians.

Ask each family member to name one Christian habit that he or she would like your family to improve or begin practicing. Give a few examples to help them along if necessary. Then pray this simple prayer, inserting the specific habits named by your family:

Dear God, there are some bad habits we'd like to get rid of; and there are some good, Christian habits we'd like to practice, such as _____ _____. Forgive us. Help us put the bad habits behind us and begin or improve some habits that make us more like your Son, Jesus. In his name we pray. Amen.

Day 3: New Learnings

When your family wants to remember something important, what helps to remind you? In many families, notes and messages attached to the refrigerator remind them of upcoming dates, important trips, or planned activities. Serving as the "community bulletin board," the refrigerator may be the place where achievements are celebrated, art work is displayed, and often-used recipes are kept—all secured with the power of magnets!

TOGETHER

In Judaism, one thing was so important that it was displayed as a reminder on the doorway of each Jew's home. What was that thing? It was a statement of a belief, called the Shema (shum-MAH): "Hear, O Israel: The LORD is our God, the LORD alone. You shall love the LORD your God with all your heart, and with all your soul, and with all your might" (Deuteronomy 6:4-5). *Shema* is the Hebrew word for "hear," which is the first word of verse 4.

Jesus considered the Shema to be the greatest of all commandments—something of great importance to be displayed, believed, and practiced (see Matthew 22:34-40). To "love the LORD your God" means to give God your utmost loyalty and affection.

(1) What things are posted on your refrigerator? If your family does not have the practice of posting things on the refrigerator, talk about where you keep your "community bulletin board" and what you have placed on it.

(2) What could you post there to remind you of God's love for us and our need to love God?

 ## FAMILY FAITH BREAK

(1) Ask a family member to read aloud Deuteronomy 6:4-9, which begins with the Shema. In this passage, Moses—whom God called to lead the Hebrews out of slavery in Egypt toward the Promised Land, which today is called Palestine—instructed the Hebrews about how to make the Shema part of their everyday life.

(2) As a family, review this passage of Scripture and name the specific instructions that Moses gave to the Hebrews.

Some Jews still follow the instructions found in Deuteronomy 6:4-9. They wear an article called a *phylactery* on their arms and head. These phylacteries contain miniature versions or reminders of the Shema or the Ten Commandments. Similarly, some Jews keep *mezuzahs*—small containers with Scripture passages—on the doorpost going into their house or apartment.

 ## TAKE NOTE

Read for yourself Deuteronomy 6:6-7. Not only are you responsible for making sure that you keep love for God foremost in your own life; you also are responsible for teaching your children to love God. That is a daunting responsibility!

The fact that you already feel some need to take this responsibility seriously is precisely why you are participating in the FaithHome experience. FaithHome is designed to help you teach a love for God to your children and, at the same time, realize a love for God in your own life.

You might want to try this simple daily exercise: As you arise each morning, think of one thing you will do that day to help your children love God. That one thing might be the same thing each day. Or it might be something that you believe will be appropriate to the events anticipated during that day. The important thing is that you are intentionally planning something specific to help your children love God. That is the best start of all!

(3) Discuss as a family how you might remind yourselves daily to love God with all your heart, soul, and might. You do not have to use phylacteries or mezuzahs; rather, think about what would help your family to remember that you are to love God fully at all times. Perhaps you might do something as simple as write the words *Love God today* on a piece of paper and attach it to your refrigerator. Perhaps you might agree to greet one another first thing each morning with the words *Good morning. Let's love God today!*

(4) Work together as a family to memorize the words of the Shema, as found in Deuteronomy 6:4-5. One way to do this is to read the passage aloud together several times. Or if your family has nonreaders, an adult can read one phrase at a time, pausing to allow the whole family to repeat the phrase together. Then see if you can say the whole Shema in unison—with your eyes closed if your Bibles are still open in front of you. Children often are better able to memorize Bible passages than adults are, so do not be surprised if your children are able to do this before you are. Learning these words from the Bible "by heart" is one way to "keep these words . . . in your heart" (Deuteronomy 6:6).

Prayer:

Prayer is a time for talking and listening to God. No concern is too large or too small to share with God. If a family member wants to pray— talk to God—about something in his or her life, take the time for that to happen. No one should feel forced to share or pray aloud. Perhaps a short period of silent prayer might work for your family.

At least offer a brief prayer, either in your own words or in the words printed here:

Dear God, help us to love you with all our hearts and with all our souls and with all our might, both today and for all our lives; in Jesus' name, we pray. Amen.

Day 4: Talking About God: In the Beginning

Today you begin reading Bible passages and talking about matters leading up to your next FaithHome group session. That session will be about God. The main point of the material you will look at over the next several days can be summed up with these words from the Apostles' Creed: "I believe in God the Father Almighty, maker of heaven and earth."

 ## BACKGROUND BASICS

Who made God? The question and answer are timeless. God is eternal, not bound by time or space. Like a circle, God has no beginning. God was not made. God is!

Who is God?

As Christians, we believe that God is the Creator (see Genesis 1:2). That single belief serves as a foundation for everything else we believe about God. The opening words of the Apostles' Creed affirm that Christians believe in God, maker of heaven and earth. To say that God is Creator is to acknowledge that God is all-powerful, having dominion over all of life. We, therefore, are dependent upon God. We must be in relationship with God in order for there to be meaning, beauty, love, hope, forgiveness, reconciliation, and wholeness in our lives. Even though we are dependent upon God, God has made us the overseers of creation (Genesis 1:26, 28); God expects us to be wise stewards, respecting and using responsibly all that God has created.

How did God make heaven and earth?

That question is not as important to ask and answer once we have determined that we do, in fact, believe that God made heaven and earth. It is important to note that Scripture does not attempt to answer the question of "how" the universe was created. Rather, the Bible addresses the questions of "who" and "why." God is the Who. God is the Creator. The language Scripture uses to describe creation is "faith language." It is absolutely true! It is not, however, scientific.

In addition to Creator, God is portrayed through a variety of images in the Bible: nurturer (Psalm 23), judge (Genesis 18:25), father (Mark 14:36), mother (Isaiah 66:13), good shepherd (John 10:11), protector (Isaiah 46:3-4), and midwife (Psalm 22:9-10). Many Christians find that one image alone does not adequately portray all that we experience about and from God. The writers of our creeds, ancient and modern, also use a variety of images to portray the richness of God's relationship with us.

Traditionally, God has often been presented through male imagery. The Apostles' and Nicene creeds, for example, speak openly of God as Father. Perhaps one reason is that Jesus often expressed his own relationship with God through the intimate title *abba*, which means "Daddy." Jesus referred to God as Father many times in the Scriptures. In the Gospel of John, he uses this image 101 times.

Jesus used other images for God as well. In his parables, Jesus portrayed God as a woman seeking a lost coin, a shepherd hunting a lost sheep, a baker kneading dough, and a generous employer. The multitude of images Jesus used can help us in our understanding of God. However, because we are human and therefore limited, we can never fully grasp the fullness of God or comprehensively describe God. Once we say everything we can say about God, mystery remains.

 ## TOGETHER

(1) Ask your family members to *think about* how they would describe or tell someone else about God using no more than five words. The words do not have to make a sentence. In fact, there are no rules about how they have to use their limit of five words.

(2) Starting with the youngest member of the family and continuing with the other family members in the order of their age, ask them to *share* their five words.

(3) Take a few minutes to share with your family your own earliest memories of hearing about God. Some persons might have heard first about God from their parents. Others might have heard about God for the first time from another relative. For still others, their earliest memories of hearing someone tell them about God might have been at Sunday school, vacation Bible school, or church camp. Some might not have heard about God during their childhood but rather learned about God as a teenager or as an adult.

 ## FAMILY FAITH BREAK

(1) Ask a family member to read aloud Genesis 1:1-5.

The first thing that the Bible says is that "in the beginning . . . God created the heavens and the earth"—all that is, all that ever has existed, and all that ever will exist.

There are actually two different, and differing, accounts of Creation in the first two chapters of Genesis. For now, do not worry about that. Do not worry either about the controversies and confusion over whether the biblical account of Creation conflicts with the scientific theory of evolution.

The main things to keep in mind and to share with your children regarding God and Creation are

- God was already there when everything began;
- God is the Creator of everything;
- Everything that exists, including human beings, owes its existence to God and to God alone;
- God considered everything that God created, including human beings, to be good. In fact, according to Genesis 1:31, "God saw everything that he had made, and indeed, it was very good."

God created you and considers the creation of you also to be good.

BIBLE HELP

The early Hebrews believed that a flat earth was situated at the center of the created universe and was surrounded above and below by unformed waters. Today we have a different, scientifically informed understanding of a round earth within a solar system of planets circling a star, our sun, within an immense galaxy, which is within an even more immense universe filled with galaxies.

(2) If you have time, explore the first account of Creation as found in Genesis 1:1–2:3. Help your children discover what God created on each of the seven days of Creation according to this account:

Day 1
- light that was separate from darkness, so that there was day and night

Day 2
- the overhead dome of the sky

Day 3
- dry land appearing in the midst of the lower waters, so that the waters became the earth's seas
- plants and trees of every kind

Day 4
- lights in the sky: the stars, the sun, and the moon

Day 5
- fish and birds

Day 6
- land animals
- human beings

Day 7
- the sabbath, which is the day God rested from the work of Creation

Extended Option:

If you have the time and the weather is appropriate, take a nature walk with your children. If a park or other natural area is nearby, take your walk there. Otherwise, walk around a block or two in your neighborhood. Make a game out of noting all the different things that God created. Talk about what it means for God to consider each of those things good.

Prayer:

Your family prayer on this day might consist of having each member of the family say at least one thing he or she is glad that God created.

Close with a prayer in your own words, or pray these words:

Dear God, thank you for creating our world and all that is in it. Thank you for creating each person in our family [say their names]. This we pray in Jesus' name. Amen.

Day 5: Talking About God: Maker of Heaven and Earth

Today's focus is on your response to this God who made heaven and earth and who also made you and your family.

 TOGETHER

(1) Take a few moments to talk about what you have learned or discussed about God so far. Ask family members how they feel when they think about, see, or experience all that God has created—including their family and friends.

(2) Discuss this question: How should we respond to what God has done to make each of us and our family?

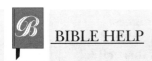 FAMILY FAITH BREAK

(1) Ask a family member to read aloud all of Psalm 100.

ℬ BIBLE HELP

A psalm is a kind of poem, prayer, or hymn often used in individual or group worship within ancient Israel (starting as long ago as 1,000 years before Christ—3,000 years before our time).

(2) Talk about the kinds of ways the writer of this psalm responded to God. For example, in the first verse, the writer calls for all the earth to praise God with a "joyful noise."

(3) Spend the remainder of your family time creating your own family's response to God, who made heaven, earth, and the members of your family. For example, you might work as a family to write your own psalm or to draw and color pictures or to take a photograph. Be creative!

Prayer:

Close your family time together with a prayer in your own words or with this prayer:

For the Lord is good; God's steadfast love endures forever, and God's faithfulness to all generations. Amen. (adapted from Psalm 100:5)

Day 6: Talking About God: Honored by Many Names

By what name do you call God? Is there one special name you should use to address God? Does it make a difference what name you use?

Most names have meaning. Often in the Bible, names are given to children—and sometimes to adults—specifically because of their meaning. For example,

Matthew means "gift of God."
Zechariah means "God remembers."
Ezekiel means "may God strengthen this child."
Nathaniel means "God has given this child."
Deborah means "bee."
Jonah means "dove."
Manachem means "comforter."
Jesus, which is a form of the name *Joshua*, means "savior"
or "one who delivers or saves."

 TOGETHER

(1) Talk with each of your children for a few minutes about how you came to name him or her as you did:

- Did you name your child in accordance with a family tradition, as in passing along a particular name or names that have been used for generations?
- Did you intentionally choose a biblical name?
- Did you name your child after a great person, perhaps in the hope that she or he might take on some of the same qualities of character?
- Did you search through one of the many baby name books available, looking for a name with just the right meaning?
- Did you select a name that passes along a particular ethnic heritage?
- Did you wait until you actually saw your child, choosing a name that seemed to fit this new being?
- Did you select a name on the basis of the way it sounds?

(2) If you do not already know what the literal meanings of your children's names are, look them up in a baby name book. Most libraries have copies; or you can buy them at most book stores, grocery stores, or discount stores. Discuss as a family whether the names of your family members, and the meanings of those names, seem to fit them.

FAMILY FAITH BREAK

(1) Working together as a family, list as many names for God as you can:

(2) Ask a family member to read aloud Exodus 3:13-15.

BIBLE HELP

As this passage opens, God has called to Moses from a burning bush that is not burned up by the fire. God is aware of the misery of the Israelites under slavery at the hands of the Egyptians. God wants Moses to lead the Israelites out of their enslavement into freedom. In today's verses, Moses asks God for God's name so Moses can tell the Israelites why he dares try to lead them out of slavery.

God's reply seems somewhat puzzling: "I AM WHO I AM." What kind of name is that?

Perhaps God was saying to Moses that God is greater than any name humans might use to refer to God. Indeed, God can never be limited to one name. God is called by many names throughout the Bible. Our English word *God* is a translation of the Hebrew words *Elohim*, *Eloah*, and *El*, as well as of the Greek word *theos*. It means exactly what god (with a small "g") means in English. "I AM WHO I AM" is usually written in English as *Yahweh* and is translated in most English versions of the Bible as *LORD*.

Other names God is called in the Bible include

Lord (*Adonai* **in Hebrew**)
king
judge
shepherd
the God of Abraham, Isaac, and Jacob
the Almighty
the Holy One
Alpha and Omega (*the first and the last letters in the Greek alphabet*)
Father (*which you will talk about during tomorrow's family time*)

(3) Talk together about one or both of these questions:

- What name or names for God help you feel God's love the most?
- What name or names for God help you feel close to God?

For younger children:

- Of all the names for God that we have talked about, which one do
  you like the most? Why?
- Which one do you like the least? Why?
- Which name or names would you like to use when you talk to God?
  Why?

Prayer:

For today's prayer, have each family member call God by the name he
or she most likes to call God, saying,

[Name for God], we praise you.

Or, if you have older children who might appreciate imagery, use this
historic prayer that was first composed by Mechtild of Magdeburg in
thirteenth-century Germany:

> *O burning Mountain, O chosen Sun,*
> *O perfect Moon, O fathomless Well,*
> *O unattainable Height, O Clearness beyond measure,*
> *O Wisdom without end, O Mercy without limit,*
> *O Strength beyond resistance, O Crown beyond all majesty:*
> *The humblest thing you created sings your praise. Amen.*

Day 7:
Talking About God:
God the Father

This last day of the first week of FaithHome looks at what it means to call God "Father." Though there are many names for God, as we have seen, understanding God as Father can help us to experience God's unconditional, parental love for each of us.

 ## BIBLE HELP

According to portions of the New Testament, at times Jesus addressed God as *Abba,* which is an intimate Aramaic word for father. Some Bible scholars say that *Abba* is more like the word *Daddy.* Much has been made in sermons, Bible study lessons, and scholarly papers of the fact that in Luke 11:2, Jesus taught his disciples to address God as *Abba.*

This teaching does not mean that God is male. Just as God is greater than any one name or collection of names, so also God is greater than gender. The second chapter of Genesis tells us that when God created human beings in God's own image, God created them as male and female.

The fact that Jesus taught his disciples to call God *Abba* teaches us something about how intimate, how familiar, we can dare to be with God. If God is "Daddy" or "Father" to us, we are part of God's family. We are immediate members of God's family—we are God's children, not just distant nieces and nephews or second cousins once removed or children who are not acknowledged the same way that the "favorite" children are. Of course, not all of us have experienced our own fathers in such a way that helps us to call God "Father" with love and adoration. We also should keep in mind that the experience a first-century A.D. Palestinian Jewish Christian or a sixth-century B.C. Jew might have had of their father is somewhat different culturally from the experience most of us have today in North America. Nevertheless, by permitting us to call God "Father," God is saying that God wants to be close to us!

TOGETHER

(1) Ask each child in your family to share his or her definitions or descriptions of what it means to be a mother and what it means to be a father.

(2) Talk with your children about what it means to you to be a mother or a father. Talk specifically about what it means to you to be the mother or father of your particular children.

(3) Parents: Later, when you are alone, reflect on how you can live out those aspects of your parenthood that will help your children get a better sense of God.

✚ FAMILY FAITH BREAK

(1) Ask a family member to read aloud Luke 11:9-13. Then, as a family, act out a brief skit that carries the meaning of this Bible passage for you. (Drama does not have to use words. If it is more comfortable for your family to pantomime the passage, by all means do so!)

(2) Use the rest of your family time to think of something that depicts the way your closeness as a family helps you better to understand God. On another sheet of paper, draw a picture, "frame" a snapshot, or otherwise express your idea.

For example, one family said that when they held hands to say grace together at family meal times, they had a sense that God wanted them to be a family, that God gave them their love for one another just as God gave them the food they were about to eat. That family depicted this sense of closeness that helped them understand God by having each family member trace his or her hand on the page in such a way that the hand tracings overlapped.

Prayer:

Close your family time by saying together—or having one family member say on behalf of all—the words of the Lord's Prayer.

FAMILY MEALS

TAKE NOTE

As you prepare for your first FaithHome family meal, remember that what and when you eat is not important. Where is important only in that you should plan for the whole family to sit down together at home; kitchen, dining room, or deck will work equally well. The important thing is to make the meal a special time for your family. There may be no better way to grow closer together as a family than to express your love for one another and for God around the family table!

Here are some tips for making your family meals stress free:

Stress-reducing Suggestions for Family Meals

- Offer food your family enjoys, but keep the menu simple. A meal does not have to be home cooked in order to build family relationships.

- Plan to have family meals at a time when all family members can gather. Invent ways to do this! Consider holding meals earlier or later—or plan a weekend brunch or dessert time. Who said family meals have to offer each of the major food groups?

- Place a white pillar candle in the center of the table and light it at every family meal. Tell the children that the candle, called the Christ candle, represents Jesus. Lighting the Christ candle is one way to remember that Jesus is a part of your life together and is always present with you.

- Pray together. If this is not something that has been a part of your family life, do not set expectations you cannot reach. Begin slowly and simply. Remember that prayer should be genuine, not forced. As you continue to make prayer a part of your life together, it will come more naturally and comfortably. Praying the Lord's Prayer together each day is a good way to become comfortable with prayer.

Family Meal #1

- Keep the menu simple. If possible, decide together what you will eat for your first FaithHome family meal.

- Follow the "Stress-reducing Suggestions for Family Meals" (see page 29).

- Light the Christ candle and say a prayer, such as this one:

Dear God, thank you for our family and for this time we have together. Help us to grow closer to one another and to you as we make faith an important part of our home life. Amen.

Conversation Starters:
- Talk about the first FaithHome session at the church and the experience ahead, inviting each family member to share her or his thoughts and feelings.

- Draw upon the "Talk Together" suggestions for the day, or make your daily "Family Faith Break" part of your mealtime together.

- Encourage individual family members to share events from the day. As the Scripture says, "Rejoice with those who rejoice, weep with those who weep" (Romans 12:15).

- Plan when you will have your next family meal, as well as this week's "Reaching Beyond the Family" activity.

Family Meal #2

- Remember to keep the menu simple!

- Continue to follow the "Stress-reducing Suggestions for Family Meals" (page 29).

- Light the Christ candle and say a prayer, such as this one:

Dear God, thank you for each person sitting around this table and for the food before us. We also thank you for the opportunity to learn and grow together in faith. Amen.

Conversation Starters:
- Draw upon the "Talk Together" suggestions for the day, or make your daily "Family Faith Break" a part of your mealtime together. Or, if you choose not to do this, use the helps below:

  - Now that we have started FaithHome and have had several days of "Family Faith Breaks" and one family meal, how is everyone feeling about them? What do you think so far?
  - What have you enjoyed? What have you not enjoyed?

- What things have we talked about or done together that have been helpful or meaningful to you?
- How can we make our daily "Family Faith Breaks" better?
- What have we learned about God? about one another? about being a Christian family?

• Make a family covenant, a promise, based on your discussion together. For example, are you finding that your daily "Family Faith Breaks" are taking far too long and are being resented by one or more family members? Decide what is realistic for your family and stick to your covenant! Share this prayer:

God, we thank you for this time together. We pray that we may discover new things about you, about one another, and about living as a Christian family. Help us find the time and energy to participate fully in this experience. Amen.

• Plan when you will have your next family meal.

 ## REACHING BEYOND THE FAMILY

During this first week of FaithHome, you have been introduced to the FaithHome experience and you have explored basic understandings of God as our Creator and Parent.

Now attempt to reach beyond your family in a "user-friendly" way! Does your neighborhood need cleaning up? Gather trash bags and start picking up litter! Pick up the litter in your own yard first. Then walk your block, picking up trash and litter as you go. Be sure to set a time limit for the experience. One family found that this first experience could go on for hours—too long for an initial outreach experience for most families. Setting a time limit will prove helpful.

At the conclusion of your first "Reaching Beyond the Family" experience, gather together. Enjoy a cold drink! Laugh! Take a photograph of your family. (Ask a neighbor to be the photographer.) And thank God for the opportunity to reach beyond your family to serve in the world.

Day 1: Talking About God: New Sharings

Today, and for the next two days, you and your family will be talking more about God, just as you have been doing for the past several days.

 ## TOGETHER

(1) As a family, try to remember as much as you can about your separate group experiences during the FaithHome session and talk about them together.

(2) Invite each member of the family to share one thing that he or she heard during the session that was new or important to him or her.

 ## FAMILY FAITH BREAK

(1) Ask a member of your family to read aloud Habakkuk 3:2.

 ## BIBLE HELP

Habakkuk is pronounced huh-BAK-uhk. It is one of the short books written by a prophet and is found toward the back of the Old Testament. The Book of Habakkuk probably was written toward the end of the seventh century before Christ. It is written as poetry, like a psalm. At the time Habakkuk was written, the great world power was Babylon. Within a few short years, the Babylonian army would conquer Habakkuk's Jewish people and destroy their capital city of Jerusalem.

The first part of today's passage praises God for who God is and what God has done. The second part asks God to continue working in Habakkuk's own time on behalf of the Jewish people, acting both mightily and mercifully.

(2) If you have very young children, you might want to focus on the first part of the passage, giving thanks that God has been made known to us.

Even if your children are older, talk about what some of the words in the Bible passage mean. They might not know, for example, that *renown* means "fame" or "how well-known someone is"; *awe* means "wonder" or "amazement"; *revive* means "to make alive once again"; *wrath* means "anger"; *mercy* means "kindness" or "taking away a punishment or harshness."

(3) Some families find it helpful to put a Bible passage, especially one that seems more difficult, into their own words. Work together to put Habakkuk 3:2 into your own words. Write in the space below:

(4) Talk as a family about how Habakkuk 3:2 is true for your time and your situation. Help your children discuss these questions on a level appropriate to their understanding and communication abilities:

- How have you heard of God's "renown"?
- How do you "stand in awe" of God's work (what God has done)?
- How has God "revived" (made alive again) God's work and made it known to you in your experience?
- How has God been kind and forgiving towards you (shown mercy)?

Prayer:

Close today's family time with a prayer in your own words or with this prayer:

Dear God, thank you for making yourself known to us. Be with and bless our family during the week to come. We pray in Jesus' name. Amen.

Day 2: Talking About God: God the Creator

Religion is the realm of the mysterious. We do not know and we can never know everything there is to know about God. There probably are some questions you would love to ask God directly if you had the chance. Your children probably have quite a few questions they would like to ask about God as well—questions that you cannot answer, questions that no human being can really answer, questions such as

- Does God ever sleep?
- Why can't I see God?
- If I can't see God, how do I know God is real?
- If God made everything and if God is good and if God is all-powerful, then how come people get hurt and get sick?
- How do I know that God really cares about me?

The Apostles' Creed reminds us that "we believe in God the Father Almighty, maker of heaven and earth." The words of this creed, like many others, remind us that we believe in the One who has dominion over all of life. To people of faith, there often is both great comfort and great meaning to be found in acknowledging that there is a God who has dominion and, therefore, One from whom we can ask guidance. We need not "go it alone," facing every temptation or trial as if it were "us against the world." We have the ability to seek guidance from One who is all-powerful and all-caring.

talk TOGETHER

(1) Ask each family member to share at least one thing he or she would like to know about God.

(2) Talk together about why each question is important to the person who shared it. Remind everyone that when your family talks together about matters of faith, there are no dumb questions.

(3) Talk about God as the Creator of all that exists. What does it mean to say that God has dominion over all of life—that God is all-powerful, having authority over all the earth? How does this knowledge about God give us comfort and hope?

 FAMILY FAITH BREAK

(1) Ask a family member to read aloud Isaiah 40:28-31.

 BIBLE HELP

Isaiah 40 was written during the period just before Cyrus, king of Persia, conquered Babylon. Years earlier, Babylon had conquered Judah and carried its leaders and skilled people into captivity. This portion of Isaiah gives hope of something wonderful about to happen for "those who wait for the LORD." The same God who is "the Creator of the ends of the earth" is also the one who will give "power to the faint" and who "strengthens the powerful."

(2) Work together as a family to make a list of what Isaiah 40:28-31 tells you about God. For example, this passage says that God is

- everlasting (verse 28);
- tireless ("He does not faint or grow weary"—verse 28);
- not completely knowable ("his understanding is unsearchable"—verse 28).

Make your list here:

(3) Learn the song "God Made the Earth," singing along with the FaithHome tape.

Prayer:

Close your family time with prayer. You can use your own words, or use the prayer printed here:

Dear God, you are wonderful. You have made so many wonderful things. You do so many wonderful things. Help us to know that you are far more than we can ever understand, which is one of the things about you that makes you so wonderful. In Jesus' name we pray. Amen.

Day 3: Talking About God: It Was Good

Children who are old enough to be self-aware frequently worry about their own worth. Faith in a good and loving God who truly loves them can go a long way toward building their sense of self-worth.

The Bible tells us that after God looked upon all that God had made, God pronounced it to be good. In fact, the Bible says God said it was very good. That judgment of goodness covers all of creation. It covers humanity. It covers every human being. It even covers your children as they wonder about their self-worth.

Children gain much of their sense of self-worth from their interactions with those around them. Those who are treated well are more likely to develop a healthy sense of self-esteem.

God has looked upon all creation and said that it is "very good." We need to look upon our children and find ways constantly to tell them that they are good—that they are loved and valued by God.

TALK TOGETHER

Family members can do much to build up one another's sense of worth. Simple words of praise and encouragement go a long way.

(1) Spend some time today offering praise and encouragement to one another. You can start this process by looking at each family member in turn and saying, "I think you are good because . . ." and then giving one, brief reason. Permit each family member the opportunity to affirm every other family member as well.

(2) If time allows, encourage family members to affirm one quality about themselves that makes them feel good about themselves. You will want to be prepared to help teens or pre-teens come up with something good about themselves. Youth often feel awkward about saying something good about themselves.

When children share something that makes them feel good about themselves, say to them, "That's wonderful! That should make you feel good about yourself." You want your children to feel good about themselves without having to rely upon compliments from other persons.

 ## FAMILY FAITH BREAK

(1) Ask a family member to read aloud Genesis 1:26-31. You might want to help younger children understand the harder words. For example, the word *dominion* means "a power over someone or something." A prince or a governor might be said to hold dominion over a country. Dominion in this sense involves power and authority; what the governor says, goes. And yet, the governor also has the responsibility to govern for the good of those within his or her dominion.

 ## BIBLE HELP

The portion of this passage that talks about the creation of human beings holds some puzzles for us. For example, in verse 26, to whom is God talking? To whom is God saying, "Let us make humankind in our image, according to our likeness"?

Bible scholars do not have a ready answer on which they agree. Some say that God is talking to the angels, to all the heavenly host. Others say that God is speaking in the "royal we," as when a queen or king says, "We shall have marmalade with our toast." Yet others have thought about how Christians believe that God is simultaneously Father, Son, and Holy Spirit and that "we" refers to those three images of God.

Another puzzle has to do with how we should understand that humanity has been made in God's "image" or "likeness." Does that mean that we look physically like God and, conversely, that God looks like a human being? Probably not. But neither is there any agreement over just what is meant here by the word *image*. Some say it refers to the spark of divine spirit, or the soul, that resides in every human being. Others say that it is the power to create or the ability to think and be conscious of oneself. Still others have different notions.

(2) Allow time for each family member to respond to this question: What in you or about you did God create?

Be prepared to allow discussion if a family member mentions something about himself or herself that God created that he or she does not like. For example, one boy expressed anger that God created him with asthma. The boy's anger was real; it also was natural for him to feel this way. If family members express negative emotions, allow those feelings to be aired while assuring the individual that God only wants good for him or her—and yet God has created a world in which illnesses and other "bad things" can cause suffering.

(3) If you have time, explore Genesis 1:26-31. Note in the space that follows what God says to the human beings God created. Put God's statements into your own, easier-to-understand words:

Prayer:

Recall the things each family member said about other family members during your "Talk Together" time. Mention them again. Say: "I thank God that . . . ," repeating what was said about each particular family member. Close with this prayer:

Dear God, thank you for making each of us the way we are and calling it good. In Jesus' name we pray. Amen.

Day 4: Talking About Jesus: The Core of Christianity

 ## BACKGROUND BASICS

Of the 110 words in the Apostles' Creed, 70 are about Jesus. Surprising? Hardly! Without Jesus Christ, there would be no Christianity. When the Apostles' Creed proclaims that Jesus was both "conceived by the Holy Spirit" and "born of the Virgin Mary," it proclaims that God willingly became completely human in Jesus while at the same time remained completely God. In the Bible we find accounts of a divine Jesus who performed miracles; calmed storms; walked on water; appeared "transfigured" beside Moses and Elijah in a vision on a mountain before Peter, James, and John; taught what was in the mind of God; brought persons who were dead back to life; and was himself raised by God from death. We also see how this fully divine Jesus was also fully human, as he was born into a human family under humble conditions; struggled with very human temptations; got hungry and ate, even after his resurrection; needed time alone to pray; cried at the death of a close friend; acted angrily at the sight of greed profaning the temple of God; and suffered and died a painful death.

Yet the most important belief we hold as Christians is not that Jesus died but that God raised Jesus from the dead. Although there is some variety in the way the four Gospels describe the Resurrection, there is complete agreement among them as to its central importance. Each writer was clear that Jesus was alive. The resurrection of Jesus was absolutely real to the followers of Jesus, not because Jesus' tomb was empty, but because Jesus was present in their midst. "We have seen the Lord," they said (John 20:25). The disciples of Jesus and a steadily growing number of persons who confessed their faith in Jesus Christ as Lord and Savior spread across the world, proclaiming with passion and conviction, "Jesus Christ is the living Lord."

In the teachings, life, death, and resurrection of Jesus, God showed the immensity of God's love and power.

 TOGETHER

Your children might know more about Jesus than they do about God. If they have attended Sunday school or vacation Bible school, much of their learning time in those settings probably has centered on learning about Jesus. Most of us who have ever had anything to do with organized religion in the church at the very least have sung the words,

> *Jesus loves me*
> *this I know*
> *for the Bible tells me so.*

(1) What do you already know about Jesus? Starting with the youngest member of your family, have everyone share at least one thing he or she already knows about Jesus.

(2) What "new" things would family members like to know about Jesus?

(3) Sing "Jesus Loves Me" together—even if you do not have young children!

 FAMILY FAITH BREAK

(1) Ask a family member to read aloud Romans 10:9-13.

 BIBLE HELP

Romans is a letter written by the apostle Paul to a congregation of Christians he had not yet met—in Rome, the capital city of the great Roman Empire. Written over twenty years after the crucifixion and resurrection of Jesus, this letter is perhaps the most complete version of Paul's understanding of what Jesus Christ means for those who believe in him.

Just prior to the passage you are looking at today, Paul has been saying that no one can live the kind of morally perfect life that would save one from death. Instead, "If you confess with your lips that Jesus is Lord and believe in your heart that God raised him from the dead, you will be saved" (Romans 10:9).

Within the context of the first-century Roman world, to say that "Jesus is Lord" meant to give your complete loyalty and obedience to Jesus. *Lord* was a political title. Modern North Americans do not have an equivalent political concept. In our democracies, while we might pledge our allegiance to our nation and follow the directions of our political leaders, we still reserve for ourselves the possibility of civil disobedience in extreme circumstances. To say that "Jesus is Lord," however, means to follow, obey, and even love Jesus without reservation.

For Paul, belief in the power of God that raised Jesus from death will bring us also to a resurrection that by the power of God overcomes our death. Within Paul's Jewish understanding, resurrection is both a spiritual and a physical matter. That which is raised from the dead is not just our souls or our spirits. Resurrection involves both our bodies and our souls. The "immortality of the soul" that some people sometimes talk about is really a concept from Greek philosophy rather than from the Bible. When the Bible talks about eternal life or resurrection, it means that God will raise our bodies and our souls together for a life that is forevermore with God. We can only speculate about what that life will be like; we can only finally say that it will be good because it is with God.

(2) Go on a "cross hunt" throughout your home. Spend five to ten minutes with each family member, searching through your home for as many crosses as you can find. You might look for

- necklaces or other jewelry with crosses;
- crosses imprinted on Bible covers;
- crosses on bookmarks used in Bibles or prayer books;
- paintings or photographs that include crosses (for example, some wedding photographs taken in churches will include a cross on an altar or Communion Table in the background);
- a first aid kit with a red cross on the cover;
- anything that has a cross on it.

Talk first about how many and what kind of crosses you found throughout your home. Then talk together about which crosses most reminded you of Jesus, as opposed to simply being a decoration or a symbol for something other than Jesus. Then talk about why the cross has become a symbol for Christians, reminding us of Jesus. (Even though crosses can be very beautiful decorations today, Christians originally used the cross as a symbol to remind them of the scandalous and painful way Jesus was put to death on a cross but was raised to life afterwards by God.)

(3) Have a family member read aloud Romans 10:9: "If you confess with your lips that Jesus is Lord and believe in your heart that God raised him from the dead, you will be saved." This is the central belief of our Christian faith. Talk about what it means to say that Jesus Christ is

Lord—to follow, obey, and love Jesus without reservation. Ask family members to respond to these questions as they are able:

- In what ways do you follow, obey, and love Jesus?
- What else could you do to show that Jesus is Lord of your life?

(4) The early Christians greeted each other cautiously by drawing a fish symbol in the dust with their foot or a stick. One person would draw an arc like this:

The other person, if he or she was a Christian, would draw another arc to complete the fish symbol:

The fish symbol meant "follower of Jesus."

Let family members practice drawing the fish symbol in pairs—on paper or in the dirt! Then adopt this early Christian symbol as your own family "greeting." Display a fish symbol on your refrigerator or "family bulletin board." "Draw" an imaginary fish symbol on the floor with your feet when you greet each other at the end of the day. Draw the symbol on notes you leave for one another. Think of as many ways to use the greeting as you like. Each time you draw it, you will be reminded that you are followers of Jesus!

Prayer:

Offer a prayer in your own words, or use these words:

Dear God, thank you for sending Jesus to show us your love and power. In his name we offer you praise. Amen.

Day 5:
Talking About Jesus:
Completely God

We who are Christians call Jesus "the Son of God." That is not just an honorary title. That is not just another way of saying that we are all "children of God." That is not just a way of saying that Jesus was a great person with divine qualities about him. It is a way of saying that Jesus, who was a human being like us, was at the same time, in some incomprehensible way, God.

 ## TOGETHER

Children are fascinated by fictional superheroes, such as those they see on television and in movies, as well as by real-life heroes, such as those on their favorite sports teams. To be sure, we often question the heroes our children choose. For example, some fictional superheroes solve problems by resorting to violence. They teach a version of "might makes right," or at least that "right should be backed up by might."

Sports heroes all too often have feet of clay or show gross levels of greed, as their names show up on crime reports or they demand extravagant payments for their talents. These people are not necessarily the best role models for our children.

(1) Ask your children to talk about their favorite "heroes."

(2) Talk about how Jesus was and is more than their favorite heroes. Jesus was

> **a real-life person and also the Son of God,**
> **who showed us what God is like,**
> **brought the love and power of God into our reality,**
> **taught us what God wants us to do, and**
> **rose from the dead so that we might live forever with God.**

 ## FAMILY FAITH BREAK

(1) Ask a family member to read aloud John 1:1-5.

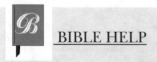

BIBLE HELP

This passage from John's Gospel talks about "the Word." John is borrowing a concept from Greek language and philosophy to talk about "the Word" as God acting, speaking, and creating. In Genesis 1, God created by speaking the words, "Let there be. . . ." That is part of the sense in which John is using this concept of "the Word." More important, for John "the Word" is Jesus.

(2) Try this experiment as a family to get a better sense of what this Bible passage is intended to mean. Wherever the words *the Word* or *him* are used in John 1:1-5, substitute the name *Jesus*. For example, the first sentence would then become, "In the beginning was Jesus, and Jesus was with God, and Jesus was God." Talk about what this way of reading John 1:1-5 tells you about Jesus and some of the ways in which Jesus is God.

Prayer:

Christians often address their prayers to Jesus. Sometimes they address God in their prayers and conclude them with words such as, "We pray in Jesus' name." Talk about what it means to you to pray to Jesus or to pray "in Jesus' name."

Then offer a prayer in your own words or in these words:

Lord Jesus, thank you for showing us God. Thank you for life. Amen.

Day 6: Talking About Jesus: Completely Human

Once we realize that Jesus is God, that Jesus is completely divine, we sometimes find it difficult to see Jesus as also completely human. One of the earliest heresies or dissenting beliefs the Christian church had to confront was the notion that Jesus was only divine and not really human.

 TOGETHER

Talk as a family about these questions, rephrasing them as necessary for the ages and communication abilities of your children:

(1) What is it that makes you a human being—and not something else?

(2) What does it mean to you to say that Jesus was completely human?

(3) In what ways was Jesus a human being just like you, and in what ways was Jesus different from you as a human being?

 FAMILY FAITH BREAK

(1) Ask a family member to read aloud Philippians 2:5-11.

 BIBLE HELP

Philippians is another letter written by Paul to a young Christian congregation. Philippi was an important city in Macedonia, now in northern Greece. Philippians 2:6-11 appears to be an early Christian hymn quoted by Paul.

(2) Try to find other Bible passages that help you think about Jesus as a human being. For example, you might mention:

Luke 2:1-7	**Jesus is born in Bethlehem.**
John 11:28-37	**Jesus weeps when he hears about the death of his friend, Lazarus.**
Matthew 4:1-11	**Jesus undergoes temptations.**

Some of the words that Philippians 2:6-11 uses to talk about Jesus' humanity include *slave, humbled,* and *obedient* to the point of death. Even though Jesus was God, he willingly became human in order to serve others and to be completely obedient to what God wanted to happen. Verse 5 introduces this early Christian hymn by exhorting Christians to "let the same mind be in you that was in Christ Jesus." In other words, we are to try to be human in the same way that Jesus was human. We are to humble ourselves in obedient service to others, even if that action costs us a lot. If we follow through completely, it might even call for our death.

(3) Talk as a family about ways you presently serve one another. For example, you might talk about cooking meals, washing dishes, cleaning the house, or setting the table for meals.

(4) Now talk about ways your family might be in service to someone outside your family. Pick one of those ways and make plans to carry out that service during the next seven days.

Prayer:

Close with a prayer in your own words, or use these words:

Dear God, we remember that Jesus was a human being just as we are human beings. Thank you for showing yourself so fully to us in human form. In Jesus' name we pray. Amen.

Day 7: Talking About Jesus: God's Only Son, Our Lord

Many Christians are uncomfortable using "religious words" such as *salvation* and *eternal life.* These are not words that we use in the course of everyday conversation. In fact, if we were asked to define these words, we might be hard pressed to do so adequately. Yet matters such as salvation and eternal life are so central to the Christian faith that we should be able to talk about them easily, especially with our children. We want our children to be able to experience salvation and eternal life. After all, that is a large part of why we want to pass along the Christian faith to the next generation.

TOGETHER

(1) What does it mean "to save"? As a family, come up with a list of as many different meanings for the words *to save* and *salvation* as you can. For example, we talk about "saving money" and "saving time." We talk about a particular baseball player being the "salvation" of his team. What do we mean when we say such things or use the word *save* in other ways?

(2) Now talk about the meanings of these words in the context of the Christian faith. We can talk about salvation meaning that we will go to heaven when we die, but that does not really cover the richness of the concept. Salvation means

- being rescued from the spiritual consequences of our sin—the evil that we do in contradiction to God's will for us;
- being healed and made whole (It is no accident that salvation is related to the word *salve* in English, something that is involved in healing.);
- being freed from slavery, as when God worked through Moses to save the Israelites from their enslavement by the Egyptians;
- being rescued from death so that we may enjoy the eternal life God wills for us;
- and much more.

 ## TAKE NOTE

How do you talk with your children about something so complicated and yet so important as salvation and eternal life? There is no simple way. These are concepts that we do not usually encounter in the ordinary moments of our everyday lives. But if we believe that salvation and eternal life are important for our children, we must at least make some beginning effort.

True, your children will not understand at first the full dimensions of these and other religious concepts. You may not understand them fully at this time either. However, if you talk with your children openly about such things, they will come to understand that these concepts are important to you and, therefore, to them as well. The attempt and the conversation are extremely important—even crucial—for the development of your children's faith foundation.

 ## FAMILY FAITH BREAK

(1) Ask a family member to read aloud John 3:16-17.

 ## BIBLE HELP

At the beginning of Chapter 3 in John's Gospel, a religious leader of the Jews named Nicodemus came to visit Jesus one night, probably so that no one would know he was talking to this controversial religious teacher. Nicodemus had a sense that Jesus had been sent by God, but he wanted to know more from Jesus about what he intended. In perhaps the most familiar verse in the New Testament, Jesus responds, "For God so loved the world that he gave his only Son, so that everyone who believes in him may not perish but may have eternal life" (John 3:16).

One very significant and comforting aspect of Jesus' words to Nicodemus is the message that God does not desire the condemnation of the world. Those who do evil in spite of God's love for them have already judged and sentenced themselves.

(2) Work as a family to memorize John 3:16. This is a verse that the great Christian reformer Martin Luther once called "the gospel in miniature." Being able to recall John 3:16 is one way of being able to keep constantly before you what Jesus Christ means for us and what Christianity is all about. If you have time, or if all your family members already know John 3:16 by memory, try memorizing John 3:17 as well.

Prayer:

Close your family time by offering a prayer in your own words, or use these words:

Dear God, thank you for sending your only Son, Jesus, into the world to show us your love and to give us eternal life. In Jesus' name we pray. Amen.

FAMILY MEALS

TAKE NOTE

In her book *Working Parent—Happy Child*, Caryl Waller Krueger encourages parents to consider the importance of eating together as a family. She writes,

> **It's a typical supper time at the Baxter house. Bill is eating like a robot, watching the sports segment on the living room TV. Marsha doesn't care about sports so she sits on a kitchen stool reading the newspaper and munching. Eddy and Freddy have left their unfinished**

plates and are busy on the family room floor with their road racer cars and tracks. For twenty minutes the parents haven't said a word. When the sports news ends, Bill pats his stomach and says, "Well, I guess supper is over."

Supper is over? To be honest, supper hasn't even begun! An indeterminate amount of eating has gone on, there's been play, entertainment, and reading, but none of this adds up to a real supper . . . .[1]

FaithHome recognizes the importance of family meals—of regularly eating and talking together as a family. The family meal suggestions throughout this *Family Guide* are intended to help you make mealtime meaningful as well as fun for your family. You will find that planning for your family meals can enrich the experience for every member of the family. Consider these questions when planning each family meal:

• Would background music be enjoyable? If so, who will choose it?

• What family member will light the Christ candle?

• Who will say the prayer?

• What family member will lead the "Conversation Starters" or "Family Faith Break" (if it is to be a part of your family meal)?

• Who will plan the menu? (*One family asks the children for menu suggestions every now and then, honoring individual requests at different meals. Menus planned by the children have ranged from peanut butter and jelly sandwiches and carrot sticks to delicious pot roast and homemade pie.*)

• Where will the meal take place? (*Once in a while you might try moving to the dining room and using the good china "for no special reason"!*)

Family Meal #1

• Let the children work together to plan—and perhaps prepare—this family meal (with adult assistance as necessary). Consider eating in the dining room and using the good china!

• Follow the "Stress-reducing Suggestions for Family Meals" (see page 29).

• Light the Christ candle and say a prayer, such as this one:

Dear God, thank you for the food before us and for those who planned and prepared this meal. We are thankful for all that you give us. Amen.

Conversation Starters:

- Talk about the planning and preparation for this family meal. Did the children enjoy being involved? What suggestions do they have for future family meals?

- Draw upon the "Talk Together" suggestions for this day, or make your daily "Family Faith Break" part of your mealtime together.

- Be sure to talk about the day's experiences and plan when you will have your next family meal, as well as this week's "Reaching Beyond the Family" activity.

Family Meal #2

It happens in thousands of homes—variations on a theme:

6:30 A.M.	Working mother leaves home for an early morning meeting at work.
7:45 A.M.	Working father transports one child to child care before going on to work.
8:25 A.M.	Older child leaves home, riding the bus to school.

In many homes, the morning's departure schedule may make it difficult for families to enjoy breakfast together. The possibility of a shared breakfast becomes even more difficult, of course, if one parent commutes a long distance to work. Perhaps this is why the weekend brunch has become popular for so many families. Brunch—and the leisurely pace associated with it—helps to provide a sense of "emotional nutrition" so often lacking on weekday mornings.

FaithHome families who feel "you described us to a T" may want to consider having breakfast at night!

- Slice some fresh fruit.

- "Iron" some waffles; fry some pancakes; or serve muffins, eggs, and bacon or sausage.

- Pour the juice or a decaffeinated drink.

- Light the Christ candle and say a prayer, such as this one:

Dear God, slow us down tonight so that we may enjoy one another and the food you have given us. Help us to remember the many people in the world

*who are without food, and help us to share with others what we have been
given. Amen.*

Conversation Starters:

- Take plenty of time to catch up on the events of the day, allowing each family member to tell about her or his day.

- Talk about some simple ways your family can "slow down" each and every day. Try to be as creative as you can!

- Draw upon the "Talk Together" suggestions for this day, or make your "Family Faith Break" part of your mealtime together.

- Make plans for your next family meal.

 ## REACHING BEYOND THE FAMILY

As part of this week's FaithHome focus, you have affirmed that God is Creator. You also have identified that God's creation is good.

We Christians affirm that God created the world to be good; in response, we want to be sensitive to the world around us. We want to know how things work together so that God's creation is preserved. Sadly, our rivers and oceans, fields and forests, are being ecologically "challenged" in a myriad of ways. While ecological "headway" can be seen in some arenas, such as the number of families routinely recycling paper, glass, or aluminum, our ecology is seriously threatened.

Plan this week to improve global ecology—close to home! Here are some suggestions to consider:

- Plant trees. Contact a local nursery for suggestions and advice.

- Develop a home recycling effort—particularly if you do not currently recycle paper, plastic containers, aluminum cans, or glass.

- Install a water-saving device on each faucet in your home.

- Educate yourself. Nearly every community has a "resident expert" in ecological concerns. This might be a park ranger, a biology teacher, or simply a sixth grader who has been recycling for some time. If you do not know someone who is an experienced ecologist in some way, visit your local library. Set your own goals for improving the ecology in your "neck of the woods."

Day 1: Talking About Jesus: New Sharings

As you begin your third week of FaithHome, take time to talk as a family about how the experience is going so far.

 ## TOGETHER

(1) As a family, try to remember as much as you can about your separate group experiences during the FaithHome session and talk about them together.

(2) Invite each member of the family to share one thing that he or she heard during the session that was new or important to him or her.

(3) What is the most important thing that has happened to your family during the past two weeks?

(4) How do you think God was involved with your family during that "most important thing"?

(5) What difference has FaithHome begun to make in the ways your family thinks about God?

 ## FAMILY FAITH BREAK

(1) Your family has spent the past four days talking about Jesus. Ask each family member to say one thing he or she has learned so far about Jesus. (Summarizing and repeating learnings can help to "fix" them in your memories for later recall and use.)

(2) Ask a family member to read aloud Mark 8:27-29.

 ## BIBLE HELP

Most Bible scholars today believe that Mark was the first of the four Gospels to be written. Even so, it probably was not written until sometime around the year A.D. 70—about forty years after the death and resurrection of Jesus! Think about how you might write today about a person or an event that changed your life many years ago. That is something like what Mark was doing when he wrote his Gospel.

Mark 8:27-29 is one of the stories that also appear in Matthew and Luke. If you have time, read Matthew 16:13-19 and Luke 9:18-20. See how these passages are both alike and different from Mark's version.

In this story, Jesus talks with his disciples about who the people around him say that he is. The disciples respond that people are saying he might be

- John the Baptist—a prophet who lived at the same time as Jesus and who was sent by God to prepare the way for the Messiah. John was killed by order of King Herod some time before the events in this story took place.

- Elijah—the greatest of the Hebrew prophets. Elijah was taken up into heaven without dying, according to 1 Kings 2. Jews believed that Elijah would return to earth just before the Messiah appeared.

- One of the prophets—in other words, someone sent by God to speak to the people on God's behalf.

Peter's own response to Jesus' question, however, was that Jesus was the Messiah. *Messiah* is the Hebrew word that means the same thing as the Greek word *Christ*. Literally, Messiah and Christ mean "the anointed one." To anoint means to pour oil—usually olive oil—over someone's head. The Old Testament tells of religious and political leaders being set apart for their special tasks through rituals of anointing. The Anointed One—the Messiah, the Christ—is the one God has set apart to bring God's kingdom to the earth. For us to call Jesus the *Christ* is to say that Jesus is the special one God has set apart to bring God's kingdom into our world.

(3) For this activity, you will need one 8½" x 11" sheet of light-colored construction paper or small piece of posterboard or cardboard for each member of your family, plus an extra sheet. If you do not have construction paper or posterboard available, substitute whatever paper you have handy. These will become place mats for each family member. You also will need markers, crayons, or other drawing utensils for each family member.

Write a different family member's name on each sheet. (Remember that you will need to have an extra sheet left over.) Give the sheets to the appropriate family members and tell them that they are not to write or draw anything on their own sheet. Pass each sheet to the right, so that everyone has someone else's sheet. Instruct them to draw something that describes the person named on the sheet. When everyone has done this, tell them to pass the sheets again to the right. Follow the same instructions. Keep repeating this process until everyone has drawn something on everyone else's sheet *except his or her own.*

Now give the sheets to the appropriate family members and have one person at a time ask each of the other family members to tell about their drawings by asking, "Who do you say that I am?"

When everyone has had a chance to tell about his or her drawings, bring out the extra sheet. Explain that this is a place mat for Jesus. Answer Jesus' question, "Who do you say that I am?" by taking turns drawing something on Jesus' place mat to describe Jesus. Talk about the drawings you have created on Jesus' place mat.

You might want to save your place mats to use with your family meals this week. If there is room at your table, set a place for Jesus.

Prayer:

Offer a prayer in your own words, or use these words:

Thank you, God, for sending us Jesus. Amen.

Day 2: Talking About Jesus: Suffered, Crucified, Buried

If your children are young, this day's family conversation may be among the most difficult. Talking about death can frighten young children. Unfortunately, many parents attempt to "hide" death from their children—and from themselves. On another note, television and films mask the finality of death for children. An actor who is "killed" in one show reappears a day later in another episode or show. It can be very confusing to children! Yet Jesus' death on a cross is central to Jesus' story and to our understanding of the significance of Jesus. Jesus' death was ugly, to be sure; however, we cannot avoid talking about it if we are to understand Jesus.

As you talk as a family today about Jesus' death, be sure to mention that his death is not the end of his story. Tomorrow you will be talking about Jesus' resurrection. Jesus' death and resurrection are both important in telling the story of Jesus.

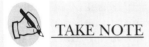 ## TAKE NOTE

If your children have not lost a relative or friend, or if you feel uncomfortable talking about death with them and are unsure of what you should and should not say to children their age, ask someone who is qualified for advice. Some persons who may be helpful are your pastor, a Hospice nurse, a school counselor, or a funeral home director. Generally, these persons have received some training in this area and have had the opportunity to reflect upon what should be said about death to children of various ages.

 ## TOGETHER

(1) Some children will have experienced the death of a close relative, friend, or pet. Often they have questions or feelings that they do not know how to answer or handle. Helping your child to understand more about death also will help him or her to understand Jesus' death. Indeed, one of the more amazing Christian beliefs is that Jesus—the Son of God—died the same death that all living things experience.

Gently ask your children if they remember the death of the relative, friend, or pet. Ask them what they remember. Share some of your own remembrances. Talk about how you miss this person or pet and what you miss most of all. Talk about feelings as well as thoughts.

If having this conversation is all you are able to do during your FaithHome time today, that is all right. This can be a very significant conversation from which many important concerns surface. Do not shortchange the time your family takes to talk about something so important.

(2) Read aloud the words about Jesus found in the Apostles' Creed.

The Apostles' Creed says more about Jesus than about anything or anyone else. More than three out of every five words in the Apostles' Creed are used to state some basic belief we Christians hold in common about Jesus. Jesus is indeed the focus of the Christian faith. What we believe about Jesus matters!

One of these basic beliefs is that Jesus—whom in previous days you have seen to be both completely God and completely human—suffered pain in the same way we might. He experienced the same death all of us will experience some day. "Jesus Christ . . . was crucified, dead, and buried."

Through the ages some persons have said that if Jesus is completely God, then he could not have possibly suffered real pain and real death. They have said that somehow Jesus' death was not really death; perhaps it was some kind of illusion. The Christian church has always fought against this opinion as a false belief. Yes, Jesus is completely God. Yet in order to be completely human, Jesus also had to suffer pain and death as completely as we do.

Tell your children that while we believe that Jesus is God, we also believe that he was completely human. In the space below, make a list with your children of things they do that Jesus also might have done:

Tell your children that two of the very human things that Jesus did in his life were to feel pain and to die. Ask your children what they think about that. Then tell them that tomorrow you will be talking about how after he died, Jesus was brought back to life by God.

 FAMILY FAITH BREAK

(1) Ask a family member to read aloud 1 Corinthians 15:1-8.

 BIBLE HELP

In 1 Corinthians 15:1-8, Paul reminded the Corinthian Christians what he had earlier taught them about the death and resurrection of Jesus Christ. Verses 3-6 probably are taken from a very early creed used by Christians to talk about and to keep in mind what they needed to believe about Jesus.

Note especially the points these verses make:

- Christ died and was buried. Although we might think this part of the creed is redundant, the early Christians were, in effect, saying twice that Christ died. He really died, and he was buried in a tomb. Unless Christ was really dead, his death had no meaning and his resurrection would not have been possible.

- Christ's death and burial were "in accordance with the scriptures." These Scriptures were what Christians today call the Old Testament. The early Christians found it necessary to ponder such Old Testament Scriptures as Psalm 69:9 and Isaiah 53:4-12 in order to understand and interpret the meaning of Jesus' death.

- "Christ died for our sins." Whether they had been Jews or pagans, the first Christians would have offered sacrifices at an altar in order to seek forgiveness for their sins. Early Christians could readily understand Jesus' death as being such a sacrifice, except Jesus' sacrificial death was for the forgiveness of all human sin.

(2) As a family, discuss what 1 Corinthians 15:1-8 teaches you about Jesus.

Prayer:

Offer a prayer in your own words, or use these words:

Dear God, it is hard to understand that Jesus really died. Help us to understand his death and prepare us to hear tomorrow about how Jesus was raised from death. In his name we pray. Amen.

Day 3: Talking About Jesus: He Rose from the Dead

The apostle Paul wrote, "If Christ has not been raised, your faith is futile and you are still in your sins. Then those also who have died in Christ have perished. If for this life only we have hoped in Christ, we are of all people most to be pitied" (1 Corinthians 15:17-19).

The most important belief we have about Jesus is that God raised Jesus from the dead. That is the event that we especially remember and celebrate on Easter Sunday each year. Moreover, the Christian church has long celebrated every Sunday as a *little Easter—the Lord's Day*.

The word *resurrection* means "a rising from the dead." Without his resurrection, Jesus would be little more than a prophet—a person sent by God to proclaim and teach God's will. Jesus certainly did that. Jesus also was a miracle worker of sorts. The Gospels tell us that Jesus performed many healings and other extraordinary, mighty works. Jesus also might be considered a martyr. He threatened the religious and political authorities of his time and place with his teachings and mighty works. The authorities arrested, convicted, and executed Jesus. But what makes Jesus more than a prophet, a miracle worker, or a martyr is his resurrection by God's power.

 ## TOGETHER

(1) How does your family celebrate Easter each year? Do you have Easter baskets? new clothes? Easter egg hunts? a large family meal? special worship services, such as one early in the morning, perhaps at sunrise?

How did your family celebrate last Easter?

(2) Discuss these questions as a family:

  - How do these ways of celebrating make your family's Easter different from any other day or any other Sunday?
  - How do you want to celebrate Easter next year?
  - What in your celebration specifically helps you to remember Jesus' resurrection?

 FAMILY FAITH BREAK

(1) Ask a family member to read aloud Luke 24:1-12.

 BIBLE HELP

Luke 24:1-12 tells one version of the first inkling that Jesus' followers and friends had that he was raised from the dead. You can read other versions of the same events in Matthew 28:1-10; Mark 16:1-8; and John 20:1-10.

The remainder of Luke 24 tells about other times when followers and friends of Jesus saw him after his resurrection. Other appearances are described at the end of each of the other three Gospels. Some of the these appearances might be the ones Paul mentions in the passage you read yesterday from 1 Corinthians 15.

The idea that someone could be raised from death seemed as incredible to Jesus' followers and friends as it might to us! Note in Luke 24:1-12 the emotions and mental states experienced by those who realized that Jesus' body was no longer in his tomb:

bewilderment	**terror**
remembrance	**disbelief**
amazement	

The first witnesses to the resurrection of Jesus were several women. Early on the Sunday morning after Jesus' death, these women went out to perform a last act of kindness for Jesus— preparing his body for final burial. Perhaps it was no accident that news of Jesus' resurrection went to persons intent on kindness. We are more likely to believe in, understand, and experience the resurrection of Jesus if we, too, act kindly when we are able.

(2) You will need a large sheet of plain paper, construction paper, or posterboard. As a family, design an Easter card on your paper. Let every family member participate in the designing and drawing. Do not worry if Easter is months away. Every day can be a time for Christians to remember Jesus' resurrection on the first Easter!

(3) Read aloud Romans 10:9: "If you confess with your lips that Jesus Christ is Lord and believe in your heart that God raised him from the dead, you will be saved." Remind your family that this is the central

belief of our Christian faith. Talk about the following questions, helping family members to understand concepts as they are able:

- Why did God raise Jesus from the dead?
- Is it hard to believe that this really happened? Why or why not?
- If we believe in our hearts that Jesus rose from the dead, what has God promised us?
- What do you think it means to "be saved"?

Prayer:

When you offer your prayer today, pray for the person or persons for whom you will be performing an act of kindness this week with your "Reaching Beyond the Family" activity (see page 74). Conclude your prayer with your own words, or use these words:

Dear God, thank you for raising Jesus from the dead. And thank you for showing his resurrection first to kind persons. Amen.

Day 4: Talking About the Holy Spirit: Pentecost

Traditionally, the Christian church has talked about God in three ways: as Father, Son, and Holy Spirit. Together, these three "persons" of God are called the Trinity. It is important, however, not to think of God as being three Gods. There is only one God. Nor should we think of God exclusively in these three ways, for God is described in many other ways throughout the Bible. Though no human words can completely describe God, Father, Son, and Holy Spirit are three very important ways that Christians have experienced God. We will talk more about the Trinity next week.

You already have spent several days talking about God as Father and Son. Today you will begin talking about God as Holy Spirit. The Holy Spirit is perhaps the most difficult aspect of God for us to think about or talk about. Our scientific, "modern" age tends to discount spiritual things as being somehow unreal. Yet the Bible tells us that our experience of a material, physical world is not all there is to our existence. Yes, life is physical; it is also spiritual. The Christian faith has to do with both the physical and the spiritual.

 ## BACKGROUND BASICS

What is the Holy Spirit? In the Bible and in other Christian writings, the Holy Spirit has been described using images such as wind, fire, and energy or force. Each of these images gives us helpful insights into the nature of the Holy Spirit.

Wind is necessary for breathing. It is sometimes gentle, sometimes forceful, and always with us. We cannot see the wind, but we can feel its presence and remain aware of its power. Likewise, the Holy Spirit is God's presence and power always, continually, in our midst. "When the day of Pentecost had come, they were all together in one place. And suddenly from heaven there came a sound like the rush of a violent wind, and it filled the entire house where they were sitting" (Acts 2:1-2).

Fire is powerful, helpful, delightful to behold, warming, and energizing. The writer of Acts records that on the first Pentecost, "divided tongues, as of fire, appeared among them, and a tongue rested on each of them" (2:3). The results were amazing! All of a sudden, communication was enhanced as believers were able to share the good news in a variety of languages, enabling persons of diverse cultures and backgrounds to hear the story of a resurrected Lord and believe. Just as the small flame from a struck match spreads in a fireplace when air and kindling come together, resulting in a roaring fire, so also the fire of the Spirit kindled the "fire" within the followers of Jesus.

Energy or force is moving, creating, life giving. The concept of the Holy Spirit as energy or force is critical within Christianity, where the Spirit is linked to "second birth." In John's Gospel, Nicodemus asks Jesus, "Can one enter a second time into the mother's womb and be born?" (3:4). In the following verse we read, "Jesus answered, 'Very truly, I tell you, no one can enter the kingdom of God without being born of water and Spirit' " (3:5). Our physical birth and our spiritual birth require force and energy!

It is important to understand that the Holy Spirit was not given for the first time at Pentecost. The first chapter of Genesis describes the Spirit's creative action: "A wind from God swept over the face of the waters" (1:2). Other passages in the Old Testament speak of God's Spirit poured out for guidance, wisdom, and faithfulness. Jesus referred to the life-giving power of the Spirit (see Luke 4:18). Later, the Acts of the Apostles celebrated the Spirit's power to gather and energize the church. So when we say, "I believe in the Holy Spirit," we are declaring again our belief in God and Jesus. The Holy Spirit is equal to God. The apostle Paul said it well: "Now the Lord is the Spirit" (2 Corinthians 3:17).

The traditional belief of Christians is in one Godhead—literally three persons of one substance, power, and eternity. The role of the Spirit within the Trinity is to energize us for faithful discipleship. The Spirit brings us assurance that the work of Christ has been entrusted to us. The very presence of God will uphold us as we do Christ's work.

 ## TOGETHER

(1) Give a grocery sack or a large plastic bag to each family member and instruct them to put any object of their choice in it—without showing the object to anyone else.

Now, with all eyes closed—No peeking allowed!—pass around the sacks and guess what object is in each sack, using your sense of touch only.

(2) When everyone has guessed what each object is, open your eyes and talk about the experience. What does God *feel like* to you? Remember, any answer is a good answer!

 ## FAMILY FAITH BREAK

(1) Ask a family member to read aloud Acts 2:1-4.

 ### BIBLE HELP

After Jesus had risen from death, he spent several weeks with his disciples. Just before his ascension into heaven, Jesus instructed his followers to wait in Jerusalem for the coming of the Holy Spirit. Acts 2 tells of what happened when the Holy Spirit came to them at the time of the Jewish festival of Pentecost. Pentecost took place fifty days after the Jewish festival of the Passover. The manner in which the Jews were to observe Pentecost is described in Leviticus 23:15-22.

(2) These are some of the things you should notice about this passage:

- The Holy Spirit came to Jesus' followers when they were all together in one place. This implies that the coming of the Holy Spirit comes to the group or community as well as to individuals. Verse 3 reinforces this idea. Although some artists have illustrated Acts 2:1-4 with separate tongues of flame resting upon the heads of the gathered disciples, a more accurate rendering would depict one central burst of fire with tongues shooting out from the center and resting upon each of the disciples. They are sharing in the same spiritual fire.

- While images of wind and fire are used in this passage to describe the coming of the Holy Spirit, we are told that there literally was a sound like the rush of a violent wind and that there were divided tongues, as of fire. Though the Holy Spirit is not wind and fire, some characteristics of wind and fire help us to think about the Holy Spirit.

- When the inspired disciples spoke "in other languages," they found it possible to communicate the good news about Jesus Christ to persons of other cultures and languages. This is not the same as the "speaking in tongues" that Paul talks about in 1 Corinthians 14 and that some charismatic Christians experience today.

Prayer:

Close by offering a prayer in your own words, or use these words:

Dear God, thank you for promising to continue to be with us in the presence and power of your Holy Spirit. In Jesus' name we pray. Amen.

Day 5: Talking About the Holy Spirit: Wind

The books of the New Testament were originally written in Greek. In Greek, the word *pneuma* could mean either "wind" or "spirit." And so it was something of a pun to describe the Holy Spirit as being like the wind in the passage you looked at yesterday in Acts 2.

Pneuma also can have the meaning of "breath." Blow out a puff of breath. That puff of breath is like a little wind. In earlier times, persons could imagine that some of a person's spirit was released through the act of breathing. And so, in Genesis 2:7, when God formed the first human out of dirt, God breathed the spirit of life into the first human and made him a living being.

 TOGETHER

(1) Take a walk outdoors as a family. At a convenient spot, stop to talk for a while. If it is not possible for your family to walk outdoors, sit for a few minutes in your yard or on a porch or balcony or by an open window.

Start by instructing the members of your family to stand or sit quietly in order to feel and hear the wind. Talk together about what it feels and sounds like. Talk about other times when the wind has been much brisker or much stiller. Also talk about

- Which way is the wind blowing?
- How can you tell which way the wind is blowing?
- Where does the wind come from, and where does it go?

(2) If there is no wind today, sit in front of a fan and turn the speed from low to medium to high. How does the "wind" feel on each of these settings? What, if anything, happened to your hair, clothes, and other objects in the room as the setting went from low to high? Ask each family member to tell what he or she likes and dislikes about "wind."

 FAMILY FAITH BREAK

(1) Ask a family member to read aloud John 3:1-8.

 BIBLE HELP

Last week you read a different portion of the third chapter of John's Gospel. You may recall that a religious leader of the Jews—a man named Nicodemus—came to talk with Jesus late one night. Nicodemus had a sense that Jesus had been sent by God, but he wanted to know more about Jesus.

In part of this passage, Jesus taught Nicodemus that a person must be "born from above"—or, as other translations say it, be "born again." Do not worry about that part today. You will talk about the new birth later this week.

For now it is enough to know that a person is born from above—born again—when he or she has experienced God's Spirit.

Verse 8 is the key verse to focus on today: "The wind blows where it chooses, and you hear the sound of it, but you do not know where it comes from or where it goes. So it is with everyone who is born of the Spirit" (John 3:8). Your walk outdoors should give you a start in understanding what Jesus was saying in this verse.

(2) Focus on John 3:8 during your family discussion of the Bible passage. Ask family members to talk about everything they can recall about their experience of the wind. Make a list in the left column that follows. In the right column, write what you think the wind tells you about what the Holy Spirit is like.

The Wind	The Holy Spirit

Prayer:

Close by offering a prayer in your own words, or use these words:

Dear God, help us to feel your Holy Spirit just as we can feel the wind. In Jesus' name we pray. Amen.

Day 6: Talking About the Holy Spirit: Fire

Fire has long been associated with God. For example, when God called Moses to lead the Israelites to freedom, God appeared to Moses "in a flame of fire out of a bush; he looked, and the bush was blazing, yet it was not consumed" (Exodus 3:2).

Yesterday, you pondered how God's Holy Spirit is like the wind. Today, you will consider how God's Holy Spirit is like fire.

 ## TOGETHER

(1) You will need a candle, a candle holder, and matches. Gather your family together. Light and place the candle in a safe place on a table where all can see it. (Keep in mind fire safety practices.) Instruct everyone to sit quietly and watch the flame for a few minutes. Then ask them to talk about what they saw. When you finish talking about the flame, be sure to extinguish it safely.

(2) Talk together about fire—what it looks like, how it feels, what it is used for, times when it is "good" (safe) and "bad" (unsafe), and more.

 ## FAMILY FAITH BREAK

(1) Ask a family member to read aloud Luke 3:15-17.

 ## BIBLE HELP

The speaker in this passage is not Jesus but John the Baptist. John was a prophet who was a contemporary of Jesus. In fact, Luke's Gospel says that John was a relative of Jesus; their mothers were related.

John spoke harsh words to the people who gathered to hear him. He judged and condemned the sin he saw around him. He called for repentance—that is, for people to turn their lives around, to turn away from sin and towards God's will for them. To signify repentance and forgiveness, John baptized them, ritually cleansing them in the Jordan River.

Because of the strong spiritual character of John, many persons wondered if he might be the Messiah sent by God to establish God's kingdom. However, in verses 16 and 17, John points beyond himself to the Messiah who will be greater than he:

> **"I baptize you with water; but one who is more powerful than I is coming; I am not worthy to untie the thong of his sandals. He will baptize you with the Holy Spirit and fire. His winnowing fork is in his hand, to clear his threshing floor and to gather the wheat into his granary; but the chaff he will burn with unquenchable fire."** (Luke 3:16-17)

Verse 17 uses farming images familiar to all who would have heard John in his time. A winnowing fork picks up wheat from the floor where it is threshed—separating the good wheat grain from the chaff, which is the stalk, dirt, and other parts to be discarded. The good wheat is gathered up; the worthless chaff is burned, just as we might incinerate trash. These are images of judgment.

Compare John's prophecy that the Messiah will baptize "with the Holy Spirit and fire" with what happened in the passage you read two days ago in Acts 2:1-4. The same Luke who wrote the Gospel also wrote the Acts of the Apostles. He knew that John's prophecy was fulfilled when the promised Holy Spirit came upon the followers of Jesus on Pentecost.

(2) Talk as a family about specific ways you have experienced fire. For example, you may have experienced fire as

- something that makes you feel warm;
- a light, such as a candle or a gas-powered lantern, that helps you see when all other power is out;
- a campfire that was part of a special time spent camping with family members or friends;
- something dangerous if it is not treated with appropriate respect;
- a useful tool for cooking food in order to nourish our bodies.

Add to these possibilities in the left column that follows. In the right column, list the things that fire tells your family about what God's Holy Spirit is like.

Fire	The Holy Spirit

Prayer:

Close with a prayer using your own words or using these words:

Dear God, warm our spirits just as fire warms our bodies. In Jesus' name we pray. Amen.

Day 7: Talking About the Holy Spirit: New Birth

One of the basic beliefs of the Christian faith is that God changes us when we surrender ourselves to God's will. When we try to do everything on our own, when we try to be "our own persons," we fail miserably. We sin. We cause harm to ourselves and others—whether intentionally or unintentionally. We place ourselves first. We think we know best, even better than God. We are selfish.

Traditionally, Christianity has talked about a "new birth" that takes place when we permit God to take God's proper place at the center of our lives. Two days ago, you read in John 3:1-8 how Jesus told Nicodemus that in order to enter God's kingdom, he would have to be "born from above" or "born again." What is this new birth?

Perhaps the simplest way to understand the "new birth" is to think about how you are different now just because you want to be a follower of Jesus. You want to do the things in your life that will be pleasing to Jesus. When you do the good, instead of slipping into careless and harmful actions, you are a different person from the not-so-good person you might have been.

For some individuals, becoming a different person after becoming a follower of Jesus happens quite suddenly and dramatically. They even know the day and place that this new birth took place for them. Other individuals have literally been born into the Christian faith and cannot think of a time when they did not try to please Jesus by their actions to some extent. Whichever way it happens, in both of these cases, persons are different than they might have been and therefore can be said to have been born anew or born again.

 ## TALK TOGETHER

(1) Talk together about what it means to be "born again." Young children in particular will need help understanding that this does not mean literally being born into the world a second time. Words and phrases such as "starting over" and "becoming new" may be helpful. Use examples of times when family members have made mistakes and have been given a chance to begin again. Or talk about making a mistake on an art project and starting over with a clean sheet of paper. You will think of other ways to communicate effectively with your children.

(2) Talk together about the things you do differently, individually or as a family, because you want to be followers of Jesus and want to please him.

 ## FAMILY FAITH BREAK

(1) Ask a family member to read aloud 1 Peter 1:3-9.

 ## BIBLE HELP

First Peter is a letter written to the Christians in several Roman provinces in Asia Minor—the region now known as Turkey. The letter probably was written sometime between the years A.D. 70 and A.D. 90. Because this time period was a number of years after the death and resurrection of Jesus (which took place around the year A.D. 30), many Bible scholars think that someone who learned about the Christian faith from the apostle Peter wrote this letter, rather than Peter himself. Whatever the case, First Peter was written to Christians in a time when Christians were threatened and persecuted for being different religiously from others around them. Christians suffered for being Christian.

To these suffering Christians, the First Letter of Peter offered hope of better things:

- God's "great mercy";
- "a new birth into a living hope";
- "an inheritance that is imperishable, undefiled, and unfading, kept in heaven";
- "a salvation ready to be revealed in the last time";
- "the salvation of your souls."

(2) Younger children will likely have difficulty understanding this passage. It is not easy even for adults to sort through. The main things to stress are that

- Christians are different from persons around them who are not Christians;
- being a Christian is not always easy or safe;
- God promises salvation to those persons who keep being Christians even when it is not easy or safe.

If your children are older, you might work together to put 1 Peter 1:3-9 into your family's own words. You can write your version in the space below:

Prayer:

Close with a prayer using your own words or using these words:

Dear God, help us to do the things you find pleasing, even when that makes us different. In Jesus' name we pray. Amen.

FAMILY MEALS

Family Meal #1

Tired from work? Stressed out from school? Home looking a little "lived in"? Put "pizazz" into a family meal by playing "beat the clock"!

- Call your favorite pizza place or other "fast food" delivery service.

- Assign each family member a simple task that needs to be done, such as . . .

    (1) Put toys and other "clutter" away.
    (2) Put a load of dirty clothes in to wash.
    (3) Straighten up one room of the house.
    (4) Load or unload the dishwasher.
    (5) Pack lunches for the next day.
    (6) Clean out the interior of the car.
    (7) Set the table—pick some flowers for a centerpiece.

Jot down other quick "jobs" you know need doing below!

    (8)
    (9)
    (10)
    (11)
    (12)

Then have each person start doing his or her task.

- Time is up when the delivery person knocks on the door or rings the doorbell. How much did you accomplish?

- Light the Christ candle. Remind family members that the Christ candle is a part of every FaithHome family meal and reminds us that Jesus Christ is present with us whenever we gather. Say a prayer, such as this one:

Thank you, God, for tasks to do, for family fun, and for the food we enjoy. Bless our family meal. Amen.

(If you do not live in a pizza delivery area, you can still play "beat the clock." Put a frozen casserole or frozen pizza in the oven. Set the timer for the correct cooking time. Be sure to stop as soon as the timer goes off.)

Conversation Starters:

- Discuss:

 - What tasks were done while we were trying to "beat the clock"?
 - What did we learn?
 - Based on this experience, what changes might we make in how we care for our home, toys, clothing, and so forth? *(One family tried this when a neighbor child was staying overnight. His response? "Gosh, I'm going to ask if we can try to 'beat the clock' at my house! If we can do all this in thirty minutes, maybe we won't need to take all Saturday morning to clean up around the house.")*

- Draw upon the "Talk Together" suggestions for this day, or make your daily "Family Faith Break" part of your mealtime together.

- Plan when you will have your next family meal, as well as this week's "Reaching Beyond the Family" activity.

Family Meal #2

Remember the old legend "Stone Soup"? The story can be told a number of ways. Here is one version:

> **A long time ago, there was a very poor family. Not having any food, they asked the folk of a neighboring village for something to eat. The villagers, however, were unwilling to share their food with strangers.**
>
> **So the strangers used their imagination to "persuade" the villagers to share their bounty. They told the villagers that "stone soup" was the most tasty soup in the world and that they had just the right stone for making "stone soup." All they needed to make the soup was**
>
> - **a large pot and boiling water**
> - **a little bit of seasoning**
> - **some diced vegetables**
> - **two pounds of cubed, lean beef**

One by one, villagers who wanted to taste the wonderful soup volunteered the needed items. Finally, the strangers added the stone—which had been scrubbed clean and boiled to remove germs, of course! When everything had simmered nicely for a few hours, the villagers lined up to receive a portion of the "stone soup." Suddenly, sharing seemed a wonderful thing to do!

For this family meal, use a crock pot to make your own version of "stone soup."

- The night before the meal, tell the story of "Stone Soup." Then let each family member choose what vegetables to add to the crock pot.

- Add water, seasonings, and meat; then put the crock of soup in the refrigerator.

- Early the next morning—perhaps just before everyone departs for school, work, or errands—plug in the crock pot and turn it to the low setting. By dinner time, the soup should be ready!

- Add rolls or sandwiches and dessert to your meal, if you wish.

- Place a few well-chosen rocks or stones around the Christ candle as a reminder that sharing is something Christians do. Before eating, light the Christ candle and say a prayer, such as this one:

Dear God, thank you for sharing your love and your Son with us. Help us to share willingly and graciously with others. Bless our meal and our time together. Amen.

Conversation Starters:

- Talk about the many ways God shares love with us, especially through the gift of God's Son, Jesus. Invite each family member to add to the list. Then ask them to suggest ways we can share with others—including ways we can share our love, time, and possessions.

- Draw upon the "Talk Together" suggestions for this day, or make your daily "Family Faith Break" part of your mealtime together.

- Plan when you will have your next family meal.

 ## REACHING BEYOND THE FAMILY

During the first part of this week, your focus was on Jesus. You explored what it means to call Jesus the Messiah and looked at Jesus as fully human and fully God. You also recalled that Jesus loved people. A hymn title says it all: "Jesus' Hands Were Kind Hands." The second verse of the hymn is a prayer and includes these words:

**Take my hands, Lord Jesus, let them work for you;
make them strong and gentle, kind in all I do.**

Remembering the example of Jesus, let your hands be kind! Bake cookies, make a casserole, or cook a crock pot of "stone soup"—whatever you want to create—and take your gift to a shut-in or to someone recovering from an illness. Or, join efforts with another FaithHome family and help to prepare and/or serve a meal at a community agency or shelter that feeds the homeless.

Day 1: Talking About the Holy Spirit: New Sharings

This week begins with more discussion about the Holy Spirit.

 ## TOGETHER

(1) As a family, try to remember as much as you can about your separate group experiences during the FaithHome session and talk about them together.

(2) Invite each member of the family to share one thing that he or she heard during the session that was new or important to him or her.

 ## FAMILY FAITH BREAK

(1) Ask a family member to read aloud Romans 8:26-27.

 ## BIBLE HELP

The apostle Paul wrote this letter while he was in Corinth to the Christians in Rome—the capital city of the Roman Empire. Paul had never met the Roman Christians; someone else had planted the Christian faith there. However, he hoped and planned to visit Rome and the Christians there after he visited Jerusalem with a relief offering and before he traveled on to the westernmost point of the Roman Empire in Spain. In this letter, we are given the most complete version of Paul's understanding of the Christian faith.

In Romans 8:26-27, Paul ponders how God through the Holy Spirit helps us approach and talk to God, even when we are weak and confused. God—as the Holy Spirit—knows what our needs are, even before we are able to put them into thoughts or words, and helps us to pray.

(2) Talk together about when you have prayed during the past twenty-four hours (since this time yesterday)—individually and as a family. What were the occasions for those prayers? Who did the praying?

(3) In the space below, write the words you use most often when you pray. One way to do this is to share some favorite memorized prayers. Another way is to share some of the words you use, such as, "Dear God," "Thank you," and "Amen." (By the way, *amen* is a Hebrew word literally meaning "may it be so.")

(4) Assure your children that even though our prayers are not always answered in the way we would want them to be, God hears all our prayers.

If you and your children do not already have regular prayer routines, such as saying grace at mealtime and praying bedtime prayers, you might learn and say together these simple and perhaps familiar prayers:

A Grace at Mealtime

> *God is great. God is good.*
> *And we thank God for our food.*
> *Amen.*

A Prayer at Bedtime

> *Now I lay me down to sleep.*
> *I pray the Lord my soul to keep.*
> *Guide me safely through the night,*
> *And wake me with the morning light.*
> *Amen.*

Prayer:

Close with a prayer using your own words or using these words:

Dear God, thank you for helping us know how to pray. In Jesus' name we pray. Amen.

Day 2: Talking About the Holy Spirit: Waiting for the Spirit

Do you find it difficult to wait? What have you waited for recently? When that something finally happened to come, was the wait worth it?

How do you spend your waiting time? Do you take a catnap? Do you fidget? Do you get bored? Do you work a crossword puzzle? Do you work on a project?

Today's focus is on waiting—waiting for the Holy Spirit. What kind of waiting is that?

 ## TOGETHER

(1) Involve everyone in making a list of times when we have to wait. Ideas might include in traffic, when someone else is occupying the bathroom, in the checkout line at the grocery store, and so on. Have fun with this activity and see how many different ideas you can list.

(2) As a family, think about one time recently when all of you were waiting. Talk about

- Why were you waiting?
- How did you decide you had to wait?
- What did various family members do while waiting?
- How hard was it to wait?
- When the waiting was finally over, was the waiting worth it?

 ## FAMILY FAITH BREAK

(1) Ask a family member to read aloud Acts 1:1-8.

 ## BIBLE HELP

You might want to compare Luke 24:44-53 with Acts 1:1-8. Keep in mind that the same person wrote both the Gospel of Luke and the Acts of the

Apostles. These two passages tell of the same event—the risen Jesus' last words to his disciples before he left them for heaven.

In his last request of his immediate group of disciples, Jesus asked them to stay in Jerusalem, to wait there until God the Father sent the power of the Holy Spirit upon them.

Verses 6-8 in Acts 1 are important to read within the context of waiting. The disciples are impatient. They demand to know whether the time has come for Jesus to establish his kingdom. They are filled with expectation. Having gathered together in the presence of the risen Jesus, they are ready. They want action *now*. They do not want to wait. "Is this the time?" they ask.

Note Jesus' response: "It is not for you to know the times or periods that the Father has set by his own authority" (Acts 1:7). God will do what God wants in God's own good time! We human beings are to wait for God. God's desires and activities are the things that are truly important. We cannot force God to act.

However, once we have waited and God has prepared us for what God wants us to do, God sends us forth. The gift of the Holy Spirit's power to us is not for our own benefit—at least not for our own benefit alone. God coming upon us as the powerful Holy Spirit is for the purpose of our going forth to witness to God in ever-widening circles.

(2) We are more impatient today—at the dawn of the twenty-first century—than were the first-century Palestinian Jews who were Jesus' first followers. We do not like to wait. We do not like time when we are not doing something we consider either constructive or entertaining. Talk about the extent to which you and your family members are uncomfortable with sitting still or being in silence. How often is your house quiet? As soon as someone enters your living room, is the television, radio, or stereo turned on?

We are so aware of time—the demands upon our time and the things we would rather be doing with our time—that we fill it up. We anticipate the next thing on our schedule even before we finish what we are doing at the moment. We sit in worship and become rather uncomfortable if the service runs overtime. We are impatient to get on with the next thing on our life's agenda. We cannot wait.

Yet there are times when we should let go of our busyness and wait. Isaiah 40:30-31 reminds us that

even youths will faint and be weary,
 and the young will fall exhausted;
but those who wait for the LORD
 shall renew their strength,
 they shall mount up with wings like eagles,
they shall run and not be weary,
 they shall walk and not faint.

Try an experiment as a family. Set aside a few minutes—between two and five minutes will do for the first time—when you will simply sit together as a family and "wait for the Lord." Set a timer for the agreed upon time, have everyone take off their watches, and sit in such a way that no one can look at a clock. Turn off the television and music. Unplug the phones for this short period of time. Just sit together; hold hands if you wish; and pray silently, asking God to be with you and your family.

Do not be surprised if one or more family members become uncomfortable, even for such a short period of time. You might want to try this experiment over a number of days, adding a half minute or so of waiting each time. Talk about what it feels like to wait in this way. And encourage family members to mention if and how they became aware of God in any way during the time of waiting.

Prayer:

Close with a prayer using your own words or using these words:

Dear God, please help us to wait, especially when we wait for you. In Jesus' name we pray. Amen.

Day 3: Talking About the Holy Spirit: One in Three Persons

We talk about God in many ways. As we noted in Day 4 of Week 3, the Christian church has spoken about God traditionally in three ways: as Father, as Son, and as Holy Spirit. These three ways of talking about God are sometimes called the Trinity. The word *Trinity* simply means something that is three things together, and yet the church's teachings about the Trinity are among the most confusing things we are asked to believe and understand about God.

How can God be three persons? Doesn't that mean we worship three Gods? If God is three persons, how then do Jesus, the Creator/Father, and the Holy Spirit talk to one another? Do they act apart from one another? How does all this work?

The Trinity is a confusing, somewhat complicated teaching of the Christian faith. Many persons would be tempted not to worry about trying to figure it out. One reason, however, that we cannot ignore this Christian teaching if we want to talk about our faith is that it is very much a part of traditional Christianity. The Apostles' Creed has separate sections, asserting how we believe in "God the Father Almighty, maker of heaven and earth," in "Jesus Christ his only Son, our Lord," and in "the Holy Spirit" (or "Holy Ghost," to use an older English word that means what we mean today by "Spirit"). There is evidence in the New Testament that the earliest Christian believers thought of God in terms of the Trinity. The Bible passage that you will be reading today talks about God as Father, Son, and Holy Spirit.

Patrick of Ireland, for whom Saint Patrick's Day is celebrated, is said to have tried to explain the Trinity by pointing to a shamrock. The shamrock is a small, green plant. Its leaves have three rounded parts extending out from the center, looking much like a "club" on a playing card. He talked about how the shamrock's leaf was at the same time one as well as three. God understood as the Trinity is something like that.

While realizing that God is greater than any words or names we might use to describe God, talking about the three persons of the Trinity helps us to remember that there are at least three very important ways that we experience and know God. We know God as

- the Father, who created us (and all that exists) and who loves us;
- the Son, who died because of human sin, was raised from the dead to make eternal life possible for us, and is now sitting at the right hand of God, interceding for us;
- the Holy Spirit, who continues to be with us, comforting, nurturing, and strengthening us through whatever life throws at us.

🎸 TOGETHER

(1) You will need paper (green construction paper if you have it; any paper will do otherwise), pencils, and scissors. *(Use scissors appropriate to*

the age of the children in your family.) Using the following drawing as a pattern or model, work together to draw shamrocks on paper—one for each family member. Write the words "God," "Father," "Son," and "Holy Spirit" as they appear in the drawing. Cut out the shamrocks.

As your family works on this project, talk about how we worship one, and only one, God. Yet we know about God and talk about God especially as Father, Son, and Holy Spirit. These three ways are not the only ways we experience and talk about God, but they are the main ways that the church has traditionally talked about God.

(2) Another helpful analogy you might use to explain the Trinity is that of water in various forms. It may begin as water (the substance of God). It may emerge as ice cubes (Jesus)—a notably different form of the same substance. When boiled on the stove, ice cubes will turn to steam (Holy Spirit)—the same substance of the same water, now released with spewing energy into the air.

 FAMILY FAITH BREAK

(1) Ask a family member to read aloud Matthew 28:19-20.

BIBLE HELP

"I baptize you in the name of the Father, and of the Son, and of the Holy Spirit. Amen."

Even today, these words used in the ceremony of baptism find their source in the commission given almost two thousand years ago by Jesus, recorded at the end of Matthew's Gospel. The words themselves are neither mystical nor magical. They are not a set formula that makes a baptism valid. Only God's readiness to accept and love a person makes a baptism valid. These words, however, indicate that this baptism takes place because God has made God's self known to us in the fullness of these three names.

Baptizing is only one of the activities Jesus asked his followers to do in this passage. Followers are also to "make disciples of all nations" and to teach "them to obey everything that I have commanded you." All Christians are given the task of helping other persons learn about and become strong in the Christian faith.

(2) Talk as a family about something that members of your family have gotten so excited about that they have wanted to tell other people about it. For example, maybe they have seen a new television show that they really enjoyed. Because they enjoyed it, they want others to see it and enjoy it as well. Or maybe one of your children has made a new friend. Because your child really likes this new friend, he or she wants to bring that friend home to meet the rest of the family so that the whole family might enjoy him or her. Talk about the following:

- What did you want to share with someone else?
- How did you tell someone else about whatever it was?
- Why did you want someone else to know about it?
- When you shared that something with someone else, did the person you shared it with have the same experience of it as you did?
- Do you think the person you shared that something with also shared it with someone else?

(3) Say that in Matthew 28:19-20, Jesus said that he wants us to talk with other people about him and to try to help them become his followers also. Talk about

- How do you feel about talking to other people about Jesus?
- If you have talked to other people about Jesus, how did they react or respond?

- If you have not talked to other people about Jesus, how do you think they might react or respond if you did?
- Think about one person with whom you might talk about Jesus. What would you say to this person?

For younger children:

- What do you know about Jesus?
- What can you tell others about Jesus? (Or, what would you like to tell others about Jesus?)

Prayer:

Close with a prayer using your own words or using these words:

Dear God, thank you for letting us know you in many ways. Help us to let others know about you. In Jesus' name we pray. Amen.

Day 4: We Are a Learning Church: Teach Them to Your Children

You want to teach your children about the Christian faith. More than that, you want to teach your children to *be* Christians. Believing in Jesus Christ is important to you. You want your children also to believe in Jesus Christ and to gain the salvation that he offers. Otherwise, you probably would not be involved in the FaithHome experience. For the next several days, you will be thinking and talking about how the church should and can help you with the task of teaching your children about the faith.

 BACKGROUND BASICS

Often when we hear the word *church*, we think of a building. Yet Scripture does not envision brick and mortar—or acrylic and steel—when it refers to *church*. The original word for church means "called" or "called out." The church is people who are called out by God for a specific purpose.

When did the church begin? Many congregations throughout the world celebrate the birthday of the church on Pentecost Sunday, which is usually in late May or early June. Yet the Christian church began long before its birth date was marked at Pentecost! It was by the action of God that the formative events of the church occurred prior to Pentecost. And it was by the action of God's Holy Spirit on Pentecost that the church began to grow.

The risen Jesus commissioned the disciples to continue his mission in the world, proclaiming the good news of God's salvation. On the Day of Pentecost, Peter preached the good news to those assembled. People responded immediately to Peter's invitation to "repent, and be baptized every one of you in the name of Jesus Christ so that your sins may be forgiven; and you will receive the gift of the Holy Spirit" (Acts 2:38).

To empower Christians fully to do the work of Christ, the church must be a learning community. The earliest believers knew the importance of instruction: "Keep these words that I am commanding you today in your heart. Recite them to your children and talk about them when you are at home and when you are away, when you lie down and when you rise" (Deuteronomy 6:6-7). Bible study, prayer, worship, and daily living in close relationship with God—each is indispensable to the forming of Christian identity.

When we understand the church as people called out by God, we begin to see that "Christian instruction" is more about interaction with other believers than it is about what happens in a particular building. In the Jewish tradition, the locus of learning was the home. We as Christians also carry that tradition. Historically, the Christian church has believed that religious nurture and instruction are the primary tasks of the home, supplemented by the rich resources of the church. Brief exposures to Christian teachings at gatherings such as vacation church school and Sunday school can never supplant the daily instruction a child receives in the home. In other words, the church's role is to assist and enable parents and others in the task of training their children in the faith.

As you prepare to lead your family in today's "Talk Together" and "Family Faith Break" times, think about what you hope your children will learn about the Christian faith. What are your hopes for them?

 ## TOGETHER

(1) Families often like to "hand down" keepsakes and memories from one generation to another. For example, one family might have a chair that family legend says was carried west by an ancestor in a covered

wagon. Another family might tell the story about how one branch of their family came to the United States in the 1880s in order to avoid being pressed into service in the Prussian army. Yet another family might point to a physical resemblance that has been passed down through the generations, such as a distinctively shaped nose or prematurely graying hair.

During this FaithHome time, hand down to your children some of those stories about your family. Maybe you can walk through your home and point out heirlooms that belonged to your parents or their parents before them. Maybe you can tell your children some interesting tidbit about one of their ancestors. If your children are adopted, maybe you can tell them something about their birth parents as well as about their adoptive family.

(2) Ask your children what they want to be sure to tell their children about the family from which they have come. List some of these things in the space below:

 FAMILY FAITH BREAK

(1) Ask a family member to read aloud Deuteronomy 4:9.

 BIBLE HELP

The Book of Deuteronomy was written to reaffirm the covenant that God had made with the Israelites after they left slavery in Egypt for the Promised Land, Canaan. Deuteronomy contains what are described as the words Moses spoke to the Israelites just before he died and they entered into Canaan under the leadership of Joshua.

In Chapter 4 of Deuteronomy, Moses urged the Israelites to remember and keep the laws that God had given to them. Among these laws were those that we call the Ten Commandments. One version of the Ten Commandments may be found in Deuteronomy 5:6-21. (Another, slightly different version may be found in Exodus 20:1-17.)

In Deuteronomy 4:9, Moses instructed the people not only to heed God's laws for themselves but also to pass on God's will to succeeding generations.

(2) Let the children take a turn at leading your discussion for a few moments. Say to them:

Pretend that I don't know anything at all about Jesus or God or the church or the Christian faith. Teach me what you think I should know.

If your children have difficulty getting started, try asking them:

What are the three most important things you think I should know about God? What are the three most important things you think I should know about Jesus?

As you allow your children to teach you in this way, several things may well happen. For one thing, you will discover to what extent they already have some knowledge about the things they need to know to be a Christian. You also might notice some things your children say that are misconceptions and that you can work to correct later on. However, for the time being, just let your children try to teach you. Do not interrupt to correct them now. Be gracious and let them continue. You just might learn something. Children often have the ability to express matters of faith in terms that adults would not naturally use. You may gain a different perspective.

For younger children:

Say:

Let's pretend that you're the (mommy/daddy/other) and I'm the child. I need to learn about God and Jesus. What will you tell me?

Prayer:

Close with a prayer using your own words or using these words:

Dear God, thank you for those things we can learn about our family and for those things we can learn from our family. In Jesus' name we pray. Amen.

Day 5: We Are a Learning Church: Learning to Do Good

The Boy Scouts of America have a motto: "Do a good turn daily." Even more than the Boy Scouts or Girl Scouts, Christians are supposed to do good. One of the big concerns of Christianity is for the way people live—the way we live as individuals and the way our actions affect others. Christians are concerned with both personal morality and social justice.

Especially as we talk about matters of morality and justice, keep in mind that children learn more from what you do than from what you say.

 TOGETHER

(1) Talk as a family about all the good things your family or individuals within your family do for others. There might be some good works that one member does that are not known even within the family.

You might begin by telling the children about how much money your family gives to the church as well as to other charities that seek to help persons. Talk about what that money goes toward doing. Do not forget to talk about the good works your church does with the money you give to it. Maybe you will need to do some research on that for yourself. Does your congregation help support the local shelter for the homeless? Does it build houses for Habitat for Humanity? Does it give money for good works through denominational agencies?

But do not stop there. Talk about the ways you do good works to help other persons directly. Maybe Mom drives for Meals on Wheels one day each week. Maybe Dad teaches a children's Sunday school class. Maybe an older sibling tutors younger students in math after school.

You can feel good about doing good works without feeling self-satisfied or self-righteous. Though there might be more you or any family could and should do to help persons in need, take time also to celebrate the good that you are doing at the present time!

(2) Now talk about the specific ways these "good works" are helping others. What might happen—or not happen—if you were not doing these things? How is God using the abilities or skills of your family members to meet the needs of others?

FAMILY FAITH BREAK

(1) Ask a family member to read aloud Titus 3:14.

BIBLE HELP

Titus and Paul were traveling companions and coworkers in spreading the gospel of Jesus Christ. Bible scholars disagree over whether the apostle Paul himself wrote this letter or whether a follower of Paul wrote the letter, using Paul's name. Whichever the case may be, the Letter to Titus was intended to give instructions for leading newly planted churches, apparently on the island of Crete in the Mediterranean Sea.

The Letter to Titus is filled with advice on what to teach new Christians about sound Christian beliefs and a distinctively Christian lifestyle. To read this advice is to gain a glimpse of the temptations that must have been present for the early Christians of Crete and elsewhere. You might read the entire Letter to Titus (It is only about two pages long in most Bibles.) with an eye toward thinking about which pieces of advice are relevant to your own set of temptations.

The writer of this letter must have thought that devoting oneself to doing good works was especially important for Christians. Not only does this advice appear in Titus 3:14; it also is expressed in Titus 2:7 and 3:8.

What are good works? Titus 3:14 suggests a definition: "Let people learn to devote themselves to good works in order to meet urgent needs." Good works meet the "urgent needs" of other persons.

One of the hallmarks of Christianity is that "good works" do not earn salvation for a person. In fact, "good works" are not really possible apart from God making them possible. Titus 3:4-7 provides emphasis for this teaching. Only God's mercy offers the possibility of salvation. Good works—"works of righteousness"—are not enough. Good works, however, are important because they are the things that a Christian, who is already saved by God's action, will naturally want to do.

(2) You and your family have already talked about the good works that your family is currently doing. Congratulate yourselves and feel good about what you are already doing!

But how many good works are enough? Perhaps the answer to that question may be seen by thinking about what "urgent needs" are still around you. Think about the specific neighborhood or community in which you live. Do not think any farther away from home than where your church or the schools your children attend are located. What "urgent needs" exist within that area?

(3) Is there any one of these urgent needs that one or more members of your family might try to meet with some "good works"? Talk about what might be possible. If there are some good works family members might attempt, map out some plans to do them.

Prayer:

Close with a prayer using your own words or using these words:

Dear God, we are glad to know that your love for us does not depend upon our ability to do good. However, we ask your help to do the good we can in order that some of the urgent needs around us might be met. Amen.

Day 6: We Are a Learning Church: Learning the Rules

Games are not much fun without rules. Without rules, someone can take unfair advantage of someone else. Without rules, there is a greater likelihood that someone will get his or her feelings or body hurt. Without rules, tempers flare as players disagree over what they are supposed to do.

A set of rules can be a good thing. Rules set boundaries. They set goals. They can serve to protect the weaker. They can let us know what we should and should not do.

 TOGETHER

(1) Try the following experiment: Get out a game that all family members can play. Depending on the ages of children, this game might be "Candyland," "Monopoly," "Parcheesi," or some other favorite. Start the game as usual; then, within a couple of minutes, play as if there were no rules. Probably someone will complain rather quickly. When that happens, stop the game. If you want, you and your family can still play the game later, using the correct set of rules.

(2) Discuss why rules are important to the game your family was trying to play. Talk about

- How did people *react* when you started breaking the rules?
- How did people *feel* when you started breaking the rules?
- What might happen in the game if there were no rules at all?
- When have you seen someone break the rules in real life—outside of a game?
- What is the difference between a rule and a law?
- To what extent are all rules or laws good?
- How do we know whether a rule or law is good?

 FAMILY FAITH BREAK

(1) Ask a family member to read aloud Psalm 119:152.

 BIBLE HELP

Psalm 119 is the longest psalm in the Bible. If you check, you will see that it has 176 verses.

In its original Hebrew, Psalm 119 was written so that each section of eight lines began with the same letter of the Hebrew alphabet. Each section in sequence would take you through the twenty-two letters of the Hebrew alphabet in order. Every line of the psalm in Hebrew contains the word *law* or a word that means something similar. The overall theme of Psalm 119 is to praise how good God's law is.

(2) Work as a family on one or both of Options A and B below:

Option A:

If you want to try a family Bible study of sorts, work together to find all the times the word *law*—or a word meaning something similar, such as *ordinance* or *commandment*—is used throughout all 176 verses of Psalm 119. You might make a list of all the words meaning "law" that you find. You also might ask each family member to say which verse in Psalm 119 is his or her favorite and to tell why.

Option B:

Talk as a family about the rules your family has. Some families have very explicit rules. Maybe some of those rules are even written down. Other families might not have specific rules, but they still have tacit— unwritten or even unspoken—rules that members of the family are expected to observe. Talk about

- How did your family rules come to be?
- How do members of your family know about the rules?
- How do the rules of your family compare with rules you know about in other families?
- What rules do members of your family complain about?
- What changes in the rules do members of your family suggest?
- What rules, if any, are rules that help make your family a "Christian family"?

Day 7: We Are a Learning Church: Not Everyone Has to Do Things the Same

Yesterday your family spent time talking about rules. Rules are usually thought of as being restrictive. They say that we have to do X and that we should never do Y. We usually think of rules as limiting our freedom, even if such limitations serve a good purpose.

The Christian faith is not entirely about rules, however. Christianity teaches much that supports freedom. Although Christians are expected to worship the same God and to give their loyalty to the same Lord, Jesus Christ, all Christians are not expected to be exactly alike.

As children participate within the life of a congregation, they will observe different individual Christians. Not all of these different Christians will behave exactly the same way. However, most members of your congregation will be living a Christian lifestyle to a greater or lesser extent. As your children observe the Christians around them, they themselves will learn how to live as a Christian.

 ## TOGETHER

(1) Talk together as a family about these questions:

- What are some ways in which members of your family are alike?
- What are some ways in which members of your family are different?
- To what extent is it important for all members of your family always to do everything exactly the same?
- If a family member looks different or does something differently from the rest of the family, do other members ever make him or her feel rejected by the family?

 ## FAMILY FAITH BREAK

(1) Ask a family member to read aloud Luke 10:38-42.

 ## BIBLE HELP

This passage tells the story of a time when Jesus visited in the home of two good friends of his—Mary and Martha. They also show up, along with their brother, Lazarus, in John 11.

As you read this brief story, think about what you think is really going on here:

• Does Jesus scold Martha for working at the many tasks that have "distracted" her, or for trying to get Jesus to criticize Mary for not helping Martha with those tasks?

• What does Jesus mean when he says, "There is need of only one thing"? Does he mean that Mary is doing the only thing worth doing? Or

might he be saying that Martha need only have done one thing—
perhaps prepared a simple meal—to offer sufficient hospitality to
Jesus?

• When Jesus says that "Mary has chosen the better part," to what
extent is he discounting what Martha has chosen to do?

The most important thing to note about this story at this time is that while
Jesus does seem to take Mary's side when Martha wants to scold her,
Jesus is in no way saying that Martha is a bad person or a poor follower.

(2) As a family, take a closer look at the story of Mary and Martha in
Luke 10:38-42 and note the things that can be said about each of the two
women. Make lists in the space below:

Mary	Martha

(3) Note that on this occasion, Jesus said that Mary was doing the right
thing—listening to what he was saying. Note also that Jesus is not
condemning Martha for fussing about her various tasks. He only says
something in response to her attempts to manipulate Jesus to get Mary
to help her.

Mary and Martha, even though they were sisters (or especially because
they were sisters), were quite different individuals. Jesus evidently was
fond of both of them (as well as of their brother, Lazarus, according to
John 11). He is not saying that Martha should become just like Mary.

Ask each family member to think of someone he or she admires
because of the way this person lives as a Christian. They don't have to say
who these persons are. Ask them to share only what they admire about
these persons and why they think they should try to imitate them in
order to become better Christians. Also talk about what they might do
differently from the persons they admire and still live well as Christians.

For younger children:

Say:

Do you know anyone who lives the kind of life you think Jesus wants us to live? (You might want to paint a picture using words such as loving, kind, giving, caring.) **What do you like most about this person? Why? Would you like to be more like this person? If so, why?**

Prayer:

Close with a prayer using your own words or using these words:

Dear God, we thank you for all the different examples we have around us of people who are good Christians. Help us to see and learn from the best of each of them. We pray in Jesus' name. Amen.

 ## FAMILY MEALS

Family Meal #1

Tell the children that because the meal they helped to plan and prepare during Week 2 of FaithHome was such a success, you'd like them to do it again! (If for some reason this was a bad experience, encourage the children to be your assistants this time around.)

- Ask the children in your home to help plan this family meal. The ground rules? The adults must eat what the children cook! Choose the menu for its simplicity and nutritional balance, taking advantage of the opportunity for a mini "nutrition lesson."

- Take one or more children with you to shop for needed items, involving them in comparison shopping.

- Help young children to measure ingredients, adding to their understanding of mathematics.

- As children prepare the meal, add to the fun by taking photographs of the "work in progress." Later, post the photos for all to see!

- When the meal is prepared, enjoy it! Compliment children on their efforts. Even if the end result is less appetizing than you might wish, your children probably will enjoy it thoroughly!

• Light the Christ candle and say a prayer, such as this one:

Dear God, long ago you gathered your loved ones around a table of food. After your resurrection, you broke bread at a simple table with two of your followers and "their eyes were opened" (Luke 24:30-31). Open our eyes to the miracle of loving one another and enjoying the gifts of food you have given us today. Amen.

Conversation Starters:

• Talk about the experience of planning and preparing this family meal. How was it different from their first effort in meal planning and preparation during Week 2? What did they learn?

• Draw upon the "Talk Together" suggestions for this day, or make your daily "Family Faith Break" part of your mealtime together.

• Plan when you will have your next family meal, as well as this week's "Reaching Beyond the Family" activity.

Family Meal #2

Church youth groups sometimes use food to help "bond" their members. Deepen your bonds as a family by borrowing an idea or two!

• Top a Spud!

Wash large potatoes with soap and water. Leave skins intact. "Stab" each potato with a sharp knife a few times to allow steam to escape during baking. Bake potatoes in microwave or conventional oven until each is fully baked. While potatoes are baking, family members should put containers of their favorite toppings on the counter. These might include shredded cheese, salt, pepper, bacon bits, tomatoes, chili, sour cream, butter, cooked broccoli, or other cooked vegetables. When it is time to eat, form a "serving line" and let each family member "top a spud."

OR

• Build a Sub!

In advance, go to a local submarine sandwich shop or grocery store and buy a *large* loaf of unsliced bread—suitable for use in a submarine sandwich. (Some specialty bread stores have been known to make bread six feet long for this "bonding" activity!) If your family is large, you may need to buy several loafs.

Encourage each family member to put his or her favorite sandwich toppings—such as ham, cheese, shredded lettuce, tomatoes, peppers, mayonnaise, mustard, roast beef, bacon, etc.—on the counter. Work together to build your "family size" submarine sandwich. When it is complete, cut portions for each family member. Add chips or a fruit salad or soup for an easy meal.

- Light the Christ candle and say a prayer, such as this one:

Dear God, you have brought us together as a family. Help us to grow stronger as a family and more loving. Amen.

Conversation Starters:

- Enjoy talking with one another about this fun mealtime experience and the day's activities.

- Draw upon the "Talk Together" suggestions for this day or make your daily "Family Faith Break" part of your mealtime together.

- Plan when you will have your next family meal.

 <u>REACHING BEYOND THE FAMILY</u>

This week, you have learned about God, the Holy Spirit. As you learn more about the effect of the Holy Spirit on the early church, you will discover that the Holy Spirit allowed the church to serve marginalized men, women, and children—the poor, the hungry, the homeless, and particularly widows in Jerusalem.

Today, many Christians are involved in ministry among the marginalized. A child makes sandwiches to distribute to the homeless along a busy roadside. A teenager organizes his school to collect winter coats and warm hats and mittens to give to those who have inadequate winter clothing. A family chooses to spend one Saturday morning per month to work in their community "Loaves and Fishes" program. A group of Christian singles hold a large party in their city each year. You can come—if you donate a pair of men's shoes to give to those in need of them. A busy mother and her four-year-old son decide to deliver "Meals on Wheels" during one lunch hour a week, forging meaningful relationships with the people who are receiving meals.

This week, explore what needs the marginalized in your community have. Discover how you can help. Begin simply; but don't back away from what could become the most meaningful outreach activity in your FaithHome experience.

Day 1: We Are a Learning Church: Obedience

Obedience. Ask any parent to name some of the things desired of his or her children, and obedience—to good laws and purposeful values—will certainly be among them. From the beginning of the Judeo-Christian faith, followers of God have wanted to know what God required of them. Through the teachings of the patriarchs, prophets, and priests, Israel was told to be obedient to the laws of God. The people were to worship the one God. They were to obey the commandments. They were to live kindly and benevolently.

Unlike many people of the time who worshiped other gods, the Jews knew that the one God desires justice for the weak and oppressed. Threaded throughout the pages of the Old Testament (and later the New Testament) are countless statements on behalf of the poor and the marginalized. This understanding set Israel apart from surrounding nations, which tended to focus on the needs of the ruling classes.

Today, it is important for Christians to know what it is that God desires. But knowledge is not only knowing about God, however important that is. It is equally important to do what God desires us to do—to be obedient. Knowledge is to emerge into righteous living. Simply put, we are to "walk the walk," not merely to "talk the talk."

 TOGETHER

(1) Spend a few moments as a family identifying some of the things you believe God desires. Encourage family members to go beyond initial comments such as, "Love each other."

(2) A refrain of a hymn says,

> **Jesu, Jesu, fill us with your love,**
> **show us how to serve the neighbors we have from you.**[1]

Talk about who your "neighbors" are—whom God wants you to love.

(3) Ask each family member to answer this question:

What keeps you from loving or serving others as completely as God desires?

The answer might be different for every member of your family. In one family of four, the five-year-old child thought meaningfully and responded, "I'm not big enough to reach my arms around people and hug them." An older child, a middle schooler, said something quite different: "I know I should give more money through our church to help people. But I never seem to have enough even for things I want to do." Responses will differ; all responses, however, can be quite meaningful.

 ## FAMILY FAITH BREAK

(1) Ask a family member to read aloud Isaiah 1:17. Define words that young children might not easily understand. For example, *justice* might be explained as "right and fair." *Oppressed* people might easily be understood as people who are "bullied" by others. Explain that widows and orphans are examples of people who, even today, may not have many material things. At the time Isaiah was writing, widows and orphans were two classes of people often subject to oppression. They were often quite powerless. Jewish laws extended special concern for their protection (see Exodus 22:22; Deuteronomy 24:17; 27:19).

(2) Talk about the example of Mother Teresa, who has challenged some of the worst injustices of our world. Many people have tried to dissuade her from her ministry to the poor and marginalized, particularly in the early days. Mother Teresa, however, has not been easily dismissed! She sees her task as a simple one. She is to serve the impoverished and the dying as willingly and gladly as Jesus served them. Her prayer is to be worthy to do this:

> **Make us worthy, Lord,**
> **To serve those throughout the world who live and die in poverty or hunger.**
>
> **Give them, through our hands, this day their daily bread; and by our understanding love, give peace and joy.**
> **Amen.**[2]

Now talk together about how your family might help extend God's love in your community, particularly among those who have few advantages. Record some of your thoughts in the space below. Perhaps it will lead you to a new way of reaching beyond your family!

Prayer:

Close by offering a prayer using your own words or using these words:

Dear God, we thank you for loving us and for helping us to love others. Every day, help us to seek justice for other people. Amen.

Day 2: We Are a Learning Church: Lifelong Learning

Most children look forward to the time when they can begin school. New book bags, sleeping mats, sharpened pencils, and crayons are proudly carried that first year. Some children are able to keep an excitement for learning throughout their school years. Others can hardly wait until they graduate. A fortunate few continue to have a love for learning throughout their lives.

As Christians, our heritage has long understood learning to be lifelong. In particular, the Judeo-Christian faith has prized the formation of character. In her book *Working Parent—Happy Child*, Caryl Waller Krueger outlines eight categories of traits parents say they want to instill in their children:

self-esteem
love
intelligence, creativity, inquisitiveness
self-government, orderliness
responsibility, poise, leadership
honesty, ethics, religious faith, patriotism
ability to communicate
cheerfulness[3]

Honesty, ethics, and religious faith can be among the more difficult traits to develop, perhaps because they are learned over the course of a lifetime.

As a family engaged in the FaithHome experience, you are spending a significant amount of time and energy at church and at home developing many of the traits outlined above *within a Christian perspective.* Why are you doing this? Perhaps it is because you value both your faith and your children, and you want your children to have high moral values that reflect a growing Christian faith.

 ## TOGETHER

(1) Your FaithHome experience is nearly half over. Take a few moments and talk about your experience:

- What were some of the reasons you began the FaithHome experience?
- What have been the most helpful aspects of the experience so far?
- What have been the most challenging/growth-producing aspects of your experience?
- In what ways have you grown closer to one another? closer to God? closer to other Christians?
- In what ways have you become wiser?

(2) Talk about the things you may be doing now as a family that you were not doing prior to the FaithHome experience. Would you like to continue doing these things? Why or why not?

 ## FAMILY FAITH BREAK

(1) Ask a family member to read aloud Proverbs 1:1-9.

 ## BIBLE HELP

The Book of Proverbs contains a series of statements designed to give the reader sound advice and fundamental values. As such, the Book of Proverbs is categorized as "Wisdom Literature" in the Bible. Throughout the book are observations on life, frequently phrased in a kind of poetic verse. In this chapter and continuing through Chapter 9, instructions are given in "wisdom poems"—a form borrowed from Egyptian literature. These poems are primarily addressing young people. The speaker or advice giver is frequently a parent or teacher, advising a child or pupil. The Book of Proverbs frequently compares such opposites as good versus evil, life versus death, wisdom versus folly, parental instruction versus peer pressure or the lure of the world.

Note especially Proverbs 1:7. In this verse the phrase "the fear of the LORD" does not mean that we are to be afraid of God. It means that we are to be in awe. Recognizing the wisdom and power of God and our proper position within creation is the basis for all true knowledge.

What parent is not pleased by verses 8 and 9?

> **Hear, my child, your father's instruction,**
> **and do not reject your mother's teaching;**
> **for they are a fair garland for your head,**
> **and pendants for your neck.**

Before we become too puffed up over such accolades, let us note that other passages of Scripture remind us that we, too, are constantly to seek God's presence so that we do not become ineffective parents and bring our children to harm!

The Book of Proverbs and many other parts of the Bible remind us that the search for knowledge and wisdom is indeed lifelong. Our relationship with God is the basis of wisdom.

(2) Ask each family member to name someone they think is wise or "smart." Is this person's wisdom primarily "book knowledge," or is it what might be called "good sense" or knowing right from wrong? What is the difference? Talk about the kind of wisdom God desires for us and gives us.

(3) What does it mean to be in awe of God? Ask each family member to tell what he or she finds awesome about God.

Prayer:

Encourage family members to pray aloud, if one or more would like to do so. If not, share this prayer together:

Dear God, help us to continue to learn about you and what you want us to do. Thank you for loving us and guiding us each day. Amen.

Day 3: We Are a Learning Church: Learning to Love and Respect God

What are some of the gods in your life? Before you too easily scoff at the question, consider what things in your life require the most time. Which things bring you pride?

Several years ago, a pastor served a rural church in a northern state. Winters were long and difficult. Children had few outlets, except for school, church, and a few organized sports. One highly organized sport was swimming. The small community, unlike so many others, had acquired a large Olympic size indoor pool and had formed a well-organized swim club for children and youth. Children and youth engaged in daily practices, which gave them healthy exercise, taught them new skills, and helped them forge new friendships. The problem? Swim meets were scheduled for weekends, Sunday mornings included. Distances between towns were long. Usually, swimmers and their families left very early in the morning and were unable to participate in Sunday school, worship, and fellowship opportunities.

The pastor, in an effort to support a wholesome activity but also provide the nurture of the church, offered to hold a midweek service and to organize Christian education to follow worship. But the effort was not appreciated. "After all," said one parent, "we have a prayer before the kids swim. And swimming is a good family activity."

The pastor could not argue that swimming was not a wholesome activity. She knew the families participating in the swim club were close. She could applaud the enormous efforts parents were making to support their children in meeting new challenges. Those things were hard to debate. She wondered, however, if swimming had not become god to some in her parish and the pool and trophies part of an altar.

 ## TOGETHER

(1) Tell the story about the swim team and the pastor to your family. Then discuss the following questions:

- What issues do you see in the story?
- What would you have done as a family?

(2) Are there gods that threaten the time you spend with God and the church? You might find it helpful to review the family calendar. Talk about the activities or concerns you have scheduled for a week or a month. Doing so might help you identify if there is an imbalance in the activities or values you hold as a family. For example, one family examined their calendar and discovered that one child—a very outgoing teenager, not old enough to drive—had become involved in so many activities scheduled for early evening that one of her parents was gone from home three or four evenings a week. Being busy had become a kind of god—and it was taking its toll on the rest of the family!

 ## FAMILY FAITH BREAK

(1) Ask a family member to read aloud Exodus 34:14 and Exodus 20:1-6.

 ## BIBLE HELP

The Ten Commandments, a portion of which you have just read in Exodus 20, provide a core of rules for God's followers. Many of the rules prohibit us from engaging in activities or beliefs that might weaken our faith or destroy our ethics. The Commandments also help to form the "boundaries" of belief so that the community of faith operates within some recognized parameters. The Ten Commandments can be found also in Deuteronomy 5:6-21.

Note that the Ten Commandments begin with the statement, "I am the LORD your God, who brought you out of the land of Egypt, out of the house of slavery; you shall have no other gods before me" (Exodus 20:2-3). Clearly, everything else rests upon this foundation. God is God. There can be no rivals. God's power is so great that it was able to withstand the greatest pressures and fight the greatest evils—even withstand the power of a pharaoh who would enslave God's people.

(2) God is the One who has given us life, who makes life meaningful, and who desires our allegiance. Talk together about the following questions:

- Are there some benefits to living life "in balance"? If so, what are they?
- What good comes out of recognizing that God is the only "thing" that demands our allegiance?

- How does being a Christian family help us keep life in balance? Does it help us remain in a right relationship with God?
- Are there some changes that we want to make in our family as a result of our FaithHome experience?

For younger children:

- What things do you think God wants us to do? How does God want us to live our lives?
- Is doing what God wants us to do a good thing? Why do you think so—or, why not?

Prayer:

Close by offering a prayer using your own words or using these words:

Dear God, life can get so busy sometimes. Help us not to lose sight of what is really important in life—you, one another, and becoming a family of faith. Amen.

Day 4: We Are a Worshiping Church: Sunday

A man said, "I am a Christian today because going to church with my parents was one of the most natural things in the world. We were active in almost every aspect of congregational life. The adults around me made me feel at home in the church. I still feel like the church is my home."

The church, like the family, is a "faith home," a home where we feel secure in the love of God and other Christians and grow to have an abundant, vital faith. As you have explored for the previous week, the church plays an important part in helping to instruct us in the faith. We are a learning church; as the people of God, we always are growing in faith.

We also are a worshiping church. As the people of God, we are to celebrate God's forgiving love and saving grace. For most Christians,

Sunday is the day of the week set aside for worship. It is the day when we gather together to give praise and thanksgiving to God and to remember and celebrate the resurrection of our Lord, Jesus Christ—which happened on a Sunday morning. (See the "Bible Help" on page 107.) Today you will begin talking about why we set aside one day each week for worship and why worship is important to us.

 ## BACKGROUND BASICS

God loves us, hears our cries, and reaches out to comfort and sustain us. We want—and actually *need*—to respond to that love. Worship carves out a time and place for us to stop and give thanks and praise to God. The biblical commandment to observe the sabbath day in order to keep it holy (Deuteronomy 5:12) is tied to our need to worship God.

Worship is adoration. Worship involves an experience of awe in the encounter with that which we cannot understand, comprehend, or even fully appreciate. Worship is more than feeling good while singing old, familiar hymns; more than getting goose bumps hearing an especially beautiful choir anthem; more than gaining intellectual stimulation from well-turned phrases in the preacher's sermon. Of course, these things take place; and our worship is enriched by them. Yet worship is more about our coming into the presence of One who loves us and our attempt to reflect back as much love as we are humanly able. Whenever worship occurs, we find ourselves drawn closer to God; and we end up adoring God.

The purpose of worship is to please God, not ourselves. Our worship is pleasing to God when we accept God's abundant love and grace, which enables us to receive God's Spirit and hear what God's will is for our lives. God's will usually has something to do with moving out into the world and serving others. Once we have accepted God's free gifts of love and grace, we are then able to share these gifts with others.

Two specific opportunities we have in worship to experience God's grace at work in our lives and in our midst are baptism and Holy Communion. Different Christian denominations and groups have different understandings of baptism and Holy Communion. Almost all Christian traditions, however, recognize both as sacraments of the church. A sacrament is an act that was instituted by Jesus for Christians to do and that uses ordinary, everyday elements to signify God's gracious actions in extraordinary ways.

Baptism is the sign of God's seeking and saving grace. The Gospels tell us that Jesus himself underwent baptism in the Jordan River at the hand of John the Baptist. At the very end of Matthew's Gospel, Jesus commissions his disciples to "go therefore and make disciples of all nations, baptizing them in the name of the Father and of the Son and of the Holy Spirit."

Some denominations insist that only persons who are old enough to make a conscious decision for themselves about whether to follow Christ may be baptized. Usually those denominations require that baptisms be done by immersion—the person's entire body is dunked under water, signifying a thorough cleansing and a drowning, a death, to the sins of this world. Other denominations insist that baptism occurs by God's decision and not by any human decision. Because God has decided for the salvation of all who seek God through Christ, these denominations permit and urge that infants be brought by their parents for baptism. Often these denominations permit baptism by one of three methods: immersion, sprinkling, or pouring.

Whether it is the baptism of an infant or the baptism of an adult, the primary focus of baptism is on what God is doing, not merely on the intent of those being baptized. Baptism declares that God's seeking and saving love knows no limits.

As in baptism, the focus in Holy Communion is on God's work. Holy Communion is the sign of God's prior work of grace as well as God's present work of grace. Although Holy Communion includes "remembrance" of Jesus' self giving through death, it is a serious mistake to limit it to a "memory meal" or a memorial to the acts of Jesus. The Greek word for "remembrance" literally means "experiencing anew." In other words, Holy Communion is an experiencing anew of God's sacrificing and sustaining love through Jesus Christ. The present power of God's sustaining grace, as well as the awesome gift of sacrificial love, are known in the symbols of bread and juice. We gather as Christ's family around the table to eat the food that nourishes us into life abundant and unto life eternal.

As we participate in the sacraments of baptism and Holy Communion and in the many other acts of worship such as singing, praying, and listening to God's Word, we celebrate God's loving presence in our lives.

 ## TOGETHER

(1) Does your family have a traditional or customary way of spending Sundays? Talk together about how you spent the Sunday just past:

- What time did the members of your family get up in the morning? Was it a different time than on weekday mornings?
- What did your family do for breakfast? Was it a different kind of breakfast than on weekday mornings?

- What did your family members do next? and after that? and after that? Were those activities different from your usual weekday activities?
- What kind of distinctively religious things did you do on Sunday? Did members of your family attend Sunday school? participate in a worship service? go to a youth group meeting?
- Do you feel that Sunday is a special day of the week? Why or why not?

(2) Some members of your family might not have the option of experiencing Sunday as a day off from work. With modern work requirements, many persons find it necessary to work on Sundays. Talk about the jobs that might require persons to work on Sundays. If one or more members of your family work on Sundays, talk about whether they have a separate "special" day that serves as a Sunday for them.

 FAMILY FAITH BREAK

(1) Ask a family member to read aloud Deuteronomy 5:12-15.

 BIBLE HELP

Deuteronomy 5:12-15 is the fourth of the Ten Commandments. You might want to compare this version of it with the one that appears in Exodus 20:8-11. In particular, note the following:

- What reason does Deuteronomy 5:15 give for observing the sabbath day?
- What reason does Exodus 20:11 give for observing the sabbath day?

Jews observe Saturday as their sabbath day. Jews who strictly observe the rules of their religion set up their lives in such a way that they do no work at all (except perhaps in true emergencies) from Friday sunset until Saturday sunset (as a day is counted in Jewish custom). The sabbath is holy—it is set aside for the worship and contemplation of God and for prayer.

Some Christians, such as Seventh-day Adventists, also observe Saturday as their sabbath day. Most Christians, however, follow the practice of the early Christian church and observe Sunday—the first day of the week, the day on which Jesus was raised from the dead—as their sabbath day. Every Sunday becomes a "little Easter." For Christians, Sunday is holy; it is supposed to be set apart from the other days of the week for worshiping and learning about God and for celebrating the resurrection of Jesus.

(2) Different Christians observe Sunday as their sabbath day with different degrees of strictness. Some persons refuse to do any work whatsoever on Sundays, even if it means financial hardship to them. For example, some farmers have allowed themselves to lose a day when they might have "made hay while the sun shined." Other families have observed the holy difference of the sabbath through such habits as not reading the Sunday comics until after the family returns from worship at church. Many Christians try to make sure they participate in worship at a church every Sunday without fail.

Talk as a family about what you will do this next Sunday in order to observe it as a sabbath day, "to keep it holy." Make plans for how it will be different from other days of the week and for how you will take time to worship God on that day.

Prayer:

Close with a prayer using your own words or using these words:

Dear God, thank you for the gift of the sabbath. Help us find ways to keep it holy and to dedicate it to you. In Jesus' name we pray. Amen.

Day 5: We Are a Worshiping Church: Praise

Celebrating the presence of God is an implied goal of the FaithHome experience. We have attempted to provide ways for you to do that at home, as a part of a larger group at church, and within worship—both at church and at home. Whenever you participate in a worship service at church, you join others in giving thanks and praise to God. Have you ever considered how you give thanks and praise to God at home? Much of our understanding of and attitude toward worship are influenced and shaped by what happens in the home.

TALK TOGETHER

(1) Talk for a few moments about worship in your church, including what a typical worship service is like and how family members feel in worship. Then discuss the following questions:

- How do we worship God—celebrate the presence of God—in our home?
- In what ways does worship in our church allow us to respond with reverence and joy? Does this happen when we worship God at home? Why or why not?

(2) Brainstorm together to think of as many ways as you can that your family can worship God at home. Your list might include ideas related to a special time when your family can gather together to sing, read the Bible, and pray together, as well as simple ways your family can celebrate the presence of God in everyday living. Choose one or two ideas and try them this week.

 ## FAMILY FAITH BREAK

(1) Ask a family member to read aloud Psalm 100.

 ## BIBLE HELP

This psalm is familiar to many Christians. It is a hymn of praise and thanksgiving, celebrating the goodness of God. Verses 1-3 call us to worship and praise, recognizing that we do so because of the many ways God has cared for us. We may not understand all the richness of the imagery. Sheep and pastures are not common to many of our lives. Here is some information that may help us understand this psalm:

> **We think of shepherds as being gentle, patient, kind—romanticizing what is in truth grueling work on behalf of less-than-intelligent animals. It is difficult to be a shepherd. Sheep are vulnerable, living prey for larger and more aggressive animals. They are stubborn, defenseless, and in need of nearly constant supervision and protection.**
>
> **Ancient writers of Scripture drew upon their knowledge of sheep and shepherding frequently. As they wrote the pages of sacred story, they mentioned sheep, rams, and lambs over five hundred times. They saw in everyday figures of sheep the true nature of human beings before God—essentially defenseless, needing constant care and supervision. . . . During Israel's darkest moments, for instance during the Babylonian Exile when the Temple and much of Jerusalem were destroyed and thousands of God's people found themselves in a foreign land, the Jews were reminded that the Shepherd would care for them, returning them in time to safe and familiar pastures.[4]**

Psalm 100 is intended to reflect our dependence upon God, God's great love for us and protection of us, and the essential goodness of God on whom we can depend—throughout all time.

(2) Work together as a family to paraphrase this psalm. If sheep and shepherding are not images you relate to easily, choose images that have meaning for you. Use different words to praise God! Young members of your family who cannot paraphrase can be encouraged to use markers or crayons to add to the project by decorating it. When you are finished, post your work on the refrigerator door or another prominent location, such as the bathroom mirror.

Prayer:

Close your time with a prayer using your own words or using these words:

Dear God, thank you for your love and care for our family. We love you! Help us to become a strong "faith home." Amen.

Day 6: We Are a Worshiping Church: Movement

If you have young children, under age six, stop and watch them for a while—really watch them. If your children are older, remember their early years. Chances are they are, or were, very active! Whether at play or at work, in worship or in dance, coming awake or falling asleep, seldom is a young child still. It is the nature of a child to move.

Many adults, parents included, become uncomfortable when children squirm and move about in the pew during congregational worship. Many churches provide for "children's church" or an extended session of study in another part of the church building during all or part of the worship service so that children will not disrupt the adult experience of worship. Of course, there are congregations in which children are invited to participate fully and actively in worship; yet in the overall scheme of things, these are rarities. Perhaps, instead of worrying over the behavior of our children as they sit in the pew or fretting over how to keep them occupied, we should examine the way we are worshiping!

One way to begin to change your own attitudes and expectations of children in worship is to involve them in energetic and joyful worship at home. A good place to start is prayer.

Have you ever taught a child to pray? You probably taught him or her to pray in the way you were taught to pray: eyes tightly closed, hands folded, head bowed. Interesting, isn't it? Prayer, which is so natural to children, becomes so unnatural when "aided" by adults who have forgotten what it is to be a child. Marjorie Thompson offers this insight:

> **The language of faith we offer children needs to include movement, signs, and acts as well as words. Young children need concrete forms of expression. Gestures such as kneeling, bowing, passing the peace, making the sign of the cross, lifting hands in praise or folding them in prayer can be helpful.[5]**

 TOGETHER

Today, introduce a method of prayer that enables young children to participate easily. Whatever your age or the ages of other family members, offer your prayers together!

(1) You will need a few pieces of construction paper of different colors. Hold up one color at a time and invite family members to thank God for something that is that color. For example, if you were holding an orange paper, you might praise God for "orange juice, fall leaves, my cat named 'Pumpkin,' and carrots." Each color will invite the prayers of young children and may be another step in "praying aloud."

(2) Work as a family to create another kind of prayer using gestures or movements. Young children in particular might enjoy giving thanks for their bodies by using each body part you name to praise God in some way (for example, shouting, singing, dancing, jumping, lifting or raising arms). Or you might choose to create motions for a simple, familiar prayer or for a prayer that you write together. Be creative!

 FAMILY FAITH BREAK

(1) Ask a family member to read aloud Psalm 150.

BIBLE HELP

Psalm 150 is a hymn of praise in which all creation is invited to praise God. Imagine the noise! Imagine the movement! Imagine the color! Everything that is alive is challenged to praise God! Moreover, every instrument that can make music is to be used in our praise. Our physical bodies, too, are to be engaged—not kept quiet while our words do the praising.

Other hymns of praise found in the Book of Psalms give us some indication of why the worshiper is to praise God. This psalm, however, offers no specific rationale. There is simply the tacit understanding that because God is God, God is to be praised!

Young children have no difficulty capturing the essence of this psalm. It has all the ingredients they use to worship God in praise. Marjorie Thompson reminds us, "Joy is the primary hallmark of the young child's experience of God; the prayer of children under age six is that of praise, thanks, and blessing."[6]

(2) Choose one or more ways to praise God during your "Family Faith Break." Here are some possibilities for you to consider:

- If you play a musical instrument (or several) or if you like to sing, praise God musically. You need not use words. You do not need a hymnal; although if you have one, you should certainly feel free to use it. If you need words for small children to use, consider substituting "Alleluia" or "Praise God" to the tune played on the instrument. Or simply play your FaithHome tape and sing along!

- If you are an artistic family, paint your praise! Post the results in the area where you gather for your "Family Faith Break."

- One family that was not terribly musical and even less artistic went into the woods near their home and gathered reminders of God's bounty. After bringing the objects into their "Family Faith Break" area, the family paused in silence to give thanks.

Prayer:

Recall some of the things you praised God for in your prayers at the beginning of this time together. Mention some of them again; then end with these words:

We praise you for all the ways you have given us to praise you, including color, sound, and movement. Thank you, God. Amen.

Day 7: We Are a Worshiping Church: Sermon

In many Protestant Christian churches, the sermon is the centerpiece of the Sunday morning worship service. In some churches, the pulpit, from which the sermon is preached, is actually in the center of the chancel area in the front of the sanctuary. (In other churches, the visual center of the worship service is the altar or the Communion Table, suggesting that the sacrament of Holy Communion has a more central place in worship than the sermon.)

The purpose of the sermon is to help listeners understand some aspect of the Christian faith. Almost always, the sermon is based upon a Bible passage. Often the preacher will tell stories and/or offer concrete ways for persons to put the ideas of the sermon into practice during the week to come.

 ## TOGETHER

(1) Where is the pulpit located in the sanctuary of your church? When does the sermon take place in your worship service? Does it always come at the same time in the service, or does the order of the service vary?

(2) What was the topic of the sermon at the most recent worship service your family has attended together? Write down what your family members can remember about it as guided by these questions:

- Who preached the sermon?
- On what Bible passage was the sermon based?
- What was the title (if any) of the sermon?
- What do you think was the main point of the sermon?
- In what ways was that main point important for you/your family?
- If you were to take the message of that sermon seriously, what changes would take place in your life?

If you have young children, talk about the children's sermon (if there was one) or whatever they remember from the service.

 ## FAMILY FAITH BREAK

(1) Ask a family member to read aloud Acts 20:7-12.

BIBLE HELP

Acts 20:7-12 tells a story about an incident that happened as the apostle Paul passed through the town of Troas (on the northwest coast of what today we call Turkey) on his way back to Palestine. In many ways, it is a rather amusing story. Think about some sermons you have endured that seemed to go on forever! And how would you like to have been Eutychus, who is now known to us only as the young man who fell asleep and tumbled out of a window while Paul was preaching a long sermon?

Note also what Paul did after things calmed down. He picked up where he had left off in conversing about the faith with the Christians gathered in the room.

Sermons are preached for the benefit of those who hear them. If you do not gain something from listening to a sermon, then that sermon has failed. Some preachers could do more to help you gain something from their sermons; they could be more interesting, more creative, and therefore less boring!

The success or failure of a sermon, however, does not depend only on the preacher! If you are a listener, you also are responsible for what takes place in the preaching and the hearing of a sermon.

(2) Talk as a family about what the various members of your family do during the sermon. Does a child draw pictures on the worship bulletin? Do you take notes about the sermon? Or do you sometimes jot down a shopping list or daydream about the afternoon's activities? Does someone fidget? or doze?

(3) Now talk about what you do after the sermon in order to capture and put into practice the sermon's message. Do you talk about the sermon in the car on the way home or over the noontime meal? Do you ask one another what you heard as the main points of the sermon? Do you talk about what difference the sermon will make for your life?

(4) Make plans as a family to do one thing differently the next time you hear a sermon so that your family is able to benefit more from it. Here are some possibilities:

- Decide to talk about the sermon for at least five minutes over Sunday dinner.

- On the way home from worship, determine and discuss the main theme of the sermon. When you get home, write the main theme on an index card for each member of the family to carry with him or her during the coming week. (If you have young children, explain the main theme of the sermon in simple terms. When you get home, have them draw a picture to illustrate it in some way; then post the picture on the refrigerator or other special place.)

- Agree that each family member who can write will take some notes during the sermon on what the sermon is about.

- Listen to what is being said instead of finding some diversion (such as making a list or doodling) during the sermon.

Prayer:

Close with a prayer using your own words or using these words:

Dear God, thank you for sending us preachers to help us understand your message and your will for our daily living. In Jesus' name we pray. Amen.

 FAMILY MEALS

Family Meal #1

• Here is a dessert recipe young children love to help make—fruit tacos! Whether you have young children or not, all ages will enjoy eating it! Whatever may be on the menu tonight, prepare fruit tacos for your dessert!

Fruit Tacos

Ingredients:
    1 1/2 cups cold milk
    1 package instant pudding (4 servings), any flavor
    1 3/4 cups whipped topping (4 oz. container), thawed
    8 taco shells
    2 1/2 cups cut-up fruit
    1/2 cup flake coconut
    chocolate syrup

Directions:
    Pour cold milk into a bowl. Add pudding mix. Beat or shake vigorously until well blended. Let pudding stand 5 minutes. Stir whipped topping gently into the pudding. Chill until serving time. Just before serving time, spoon an equal amount of pudding mixture into each taco shell. Top with fruit and coconut.
    Pour a "smidgen" of chocolate syrup over filling.[7]

• Light the Christ candle at the beginning of your meal and say a prayer, such as this one:

We praise you, God, for the sweet things in life! Amen.

Conversation Starters:

• Draw upon the "Talk Together" suggestions for this day, or make your daily "Family Faith Break" part of your mealtime together.

• Talk about the day's events and make plans for your next family meal, as well as for your "Reaching Beyond the Family" activity.

Family Meal #2

Even humdrum meals are special when children help to create a part of them. For your next family meal, invite children to help you make "Buried Treasures" desserts and use them to bring the hidden treasures of family life to light.

• Plan a simple, nutritious meal; and follow this simple recipe for a sweet ending:

Buried Treasures

Ingredients: "Treasures" such as broken cookies, miniature marshmallows, peanut butter, fruit pieces, chocolate chips
2 cups cold milk
1 package instant pudding (4 servings), any flavor

Directions:

Choose different "treasures" to "bury"—about 2 teaspoons of each treasure. Put a treasure in the bottom of each dessert dish.
Pour 2 cups cold milk into a shaker or bowl. Add pudding mix. Shake hard for about 1 minute, or use a beater to mix well. Spoon pudding into dessert dishes, covering the "treasures." Pudding will thicken in about 5 minutes. Chill until ready to serve. As you eat, enjoy "finding" the buried treasures![8]

• Before the meal, remember to light the Christ candle and to say a prayer, such as this one:

Dear God, we have so much to be thankful for, especially our family. Help us to be aware of the many "treasures" you give us every day. Amen.

Conversation Starters:

- What "buried treasures" are a part of your family life? Talk about them as you eat your buried treasures desserts! (When a children's Sunday school class prepared this recipe and talked about "buried treasures," an astute fifth grader, who recently was placed in an adequate foster home situation where she finally felt safe and cared for, said, "I'm not sure if I'm the treasure in my new family or if my new family is my 'buried treasure.' Both of us struck gold!") Share this prayer:

Thank you, God, for the rich treasure of family life. Amen.

- Draw upon the "Talk Together" suggestions for this day, or make your daily "Family Faith Break" part of your mealtime together.

- Plan when you will have your next family meal.

 ## REACHING BEYOND THE FAMILY

During the first part of this week you explored the nature of the church as a learning community. It is obvious that the church is important to you or you would not be participating in the FaithHome experience which has been made possible through the church.

Reach beyond your own family—the "domestic church"—to your church family—the "communal church." Ask a staff member or lay leadership team for suggestions of tasks that need to be done. Here are some possibilities to get your own ideas flowing:

- Select a storeroom that requires a good cleaning.
- Mark, file, and store choir anthems and other musical scores.
- Paint classroom furniture.
- Polish pews and tidy the sanctuary.
- Fold bulletins or newsletters.
- Rake the church lawn or do other landscaping tasks.
- Visit an older member of your congregation who may feel lonely or "cut off" from the congregation.

Day 1: We Are a Worshiping Church: The Ritual of Baptism

Worship is replete with ritual. It makes no difference whether you worship at home alone or with your family or with a congregation; ritual helps to make our worship meaningful. We will talk more about the importance of ritual in the home in Week 9; for now let us consider the rituals of congregational worship, giving particular attention to the rituals of baptism and Holy Communion. Today we focus on the ritual of baptism.

TOGETHER

(1) As a family, try to remember as much as you can about your separate group experiences during the FaithHome session and talk about them together.

(2) Invite each member of the family to share one thing that he or she heard during the session that was new or important to him or her.

(3) You are now beginning your sixth week of FaithHome. Take the time to talk as a family about your experience:

- What is the most important thing that has happened to your family during the past week?
- How do you think God was involved with your family during that "most important thing"?
- What difference has FaithHome made in the ways your family thinks about God?

(4) What specific worship rituals do members of your family find very meaningful? What is it about these rituals that helps to make worship more meaningful?

(5) What do family members find special or meaningful about the ritual of baptism? If you and/or members of your family have been baptized, talk about what you know about the occasion of your baptisms. In those families where children were baptized as infants, this would be a good time to talk about what happened at the time of their baptisms:

- Where and when did the baptism take place?
- Who was the pastor who performed the baptism?
- What family members and special friends of the family were present for the baptism?
- What did the child wear for the baptism?
- Were there any interesting things that happened in connection with the baptism? *(For example, one family tells a humorous story about the baptism of an infant son. It seems that immediately before the part of the worship service when the baptism would occur, his father was swinging him in a baby carrier. Because the baby was not fastened securely in the carrier, he slipped out and landed under the pew on the blankets in which he was bundled. Even when the congregation gasped, he never awakened. The baptism itself proceeded uneventfully, except for the bright red embarrassed face of the father!)*

In addition, if any items commemorating the baptisms are available, bring them out. For example, some families might be able to show their children baptismal gowns, certificates, or candles.

(6) If one or more members of your family have not been baptized, talk about whether it is time to seek to be baptized. Factors to consider include the customs and understandings of baptism held by your congregation, your family's traditions concerning baptism, and the readiness of the individual or family for the baptism to take place.

 ## FAMILY FAITH BREAK

(1) Ask a family member to read aloud Acts 2:37-42.

 ## BIBLE HELP

This passage tells the story of the first converts to Christianity as they responded to Peter's first sermon on the Day of Pentecost. This sermon contains the essence of Luke's understanding of the Christian message and the appropriate response to it.

Those who heard Peter's sermon wanted to get to the "Now what?" Peter's reply was fourfold (though elsewhere in Acts the following points do not occur in any particular order):

Repent (turn your life around, away from sin and towards God's will).
Be baptized.
Receive forgiveness of your sins.
Receive the gift of the Holy Spirit.

(2) If all your family members have been baptized, talk about the ways that the four responses to Peter's sermon are present and apparent in your lives.

(3) If one or more of your family members have not been baptized, talk together about the difference being baptized would make in the lives of the individuals and in the life of the family as a whole.

Prayer:

Close with a prayer using your own words or using these words:

Dear God, thank you for our baptisms and for the possibility of being baptized. We rejoice in the forgiveness of our sins and in the gift of your Holy Spirit. In Jesus' name we pray. Amen.

Day 2: We Are a Worshiping Church: The Ritual of Holy Communion

Another important ritual that gives our worship great meaning is Holy Communion. Unlike baptism, which in most churches is a one-time occurrence (although a few Christian groups rebaptize in response to a significantly new conversion experience in the life of an individual), Holy Communion—also called the Lord's Supper or the Eucharist—is intended to be observed more frequently. Different denominations and even different congregations within a denomination have different customs concerning the frequency of observing the Lord's Supper. In the Roman Catholic Church, priests are expected to celebrate Mass—the Catholic Eucharist—daily. The Disciples of Christ celebrate Communion at every Sunday morning worship service. Other churches might celebrate Communion once a month or once a quarter

TOGETHER

(1) Spend some time talking about the special meal you have periodically at church. Use the words you normally hear in your congregation to describe the meal, words such as Holy Communion, Last Supper, Lord's Supper, or Eucharist. Talk about how often your church shares this meal and how it is done—whether persons come to the Communion rail or altar or are served in the pew. In particular, you will want to talk about the customs or practices in your congregation regarding the age when a person may receive Holy Communion. Answer any questions your children have.

(2) Make a note on a family calendar of the next time your congregation will celebrate the Lord's Supper. If you do not know when that will be, ask your pastor or your church's office staff. Make plans to attend as a family and to observe what you experience during the Lord's Supper.

 FAMILY FAITH BREAK

(1) Ask a family member to read aloud Matthew 26:26-30, the story of the Last Supper, and then 1 Corinthians 11:23-26.

 BIBLE HELP

The passage in Matthew begins by describing the normal ritual that the head of a Jewish household would perform at the beginning of the Passover meal. (See also Matthew 14:19, where similar words are used in the story of the feeding of the multitudes.) Clearly, Jesus is the host of this Passover meal. A change in the ritual comes with his words, "Take, eat; this is my body" (26:26), and "Drink from it, all of you; for this is my blood of the covenant, which is poured out for many for the forgiveness of sins" (26:27-28).

The words and actions Jesus chooses are tied to some other rituals in the Jewish faith. Jews were forbidden by the dietary codes from drinking blood (see Leviticus 17:10-14); but blood was used to affirm a covenant, as in Exodus 24:1-8. Jesus may be indicating, therefore, that his blood will be a sign of a new covenant as well as a sacrifice.

Because Paul wrote his letters before any of the Gospels were written, 1 Corinthians 11:23-26 is actually the earliest account we have concerning the institution of the Lord's Supper. It is noteworthy that Paul claims to have received this tradition about the Lord's Supper "from the Lord" himself, even though they never met face-to-face according to the Gospel accounts. Paul was not present for the "Last Supper," which is the model for all subsequent observances of the Lord's Supper. In any case, the tradition that Paul hands on concerning the observance of the Lord's Supper is one of the most precious heritages of the Christian faith.

Note also that according to Paul, Christians are to celebrate the Lord's Supper for two purposes: (1) to remember Jesus as he asked us to do and (2) to "proclaim the Lord's death until he comes" (1 Corinthians 11:26)—meaning until Christ comes again to the world in the Second Coming.

(2) Discuss how individual family members understand Holy Communion. What is its purpose? What aspects of the sacrament help you to worship or to experience forgiveness? (Talk in very basic terms about God's love and forgiveness with young children.)

(3) As with baptism, different Christian denominations and groups also have different understandings about what occurs during the Lord's Supper. Roman Catholics understand the Eucharist as a reenactment of the sacrifice of Jesus on the cross. When the priest intones the words, "This is my body" and "This is my blood" over the bread and the wine, Roman Catholics believe that those elements actually become the real body and real blood of Jesus Christ. Lutherans believe that in the Lord's Supper, the real body and real blood co-exist with the bread and wine that remain as they were. Other Christians, such as United Methodists and Presbyterians, believe that in the Lord's Supper we remember or commemorate Jesus' death and resurrection. If you do not already know, find out what is your congregation's understanding about the Lord's Supper and talk about this as a family. (If you need more information, ask your pastor.)

Prayer:

Close with a prayer using your own words or using these words:

Dear God, help us to remember Jesus through sharing in the Lord's Supper. Help us also to proclaim his death and resurrection, looking forward to when he returns. In Jesus' name we pray. Amen.

Day 3: We Are a Worshiping Church: Offering

During most worship services, there is a time for collecting an offering. Most churches expect worshipers to offer money for the purpose of furthering God's work through the congregation. When the ushers have finished passing the offering plates, they usually bring the plates forward to be placed on the altar or Communion Table. In many churches, the congregation sings "Praise God, from Whom All Blessings Flow" at this time.

There are several clues here to what the offering is supposed to be about. Yes, the offering is given by individuals and families and received by the congregation in order to provide funding for the various ministries of the church and for the maintenance of the physical structures of the church. Beginning tomorrow, we will talk more about our responsibilities of giving and serving.

The offering, however, is also about sacrifice and praise. Before the Jerusalem Temple was finally destroyed in the first century after Christ's birth, Jews offered sacrifices of animals, grain, and olive oil to God. The Temple priests were supported by a portion of these sacrifices, but mostly the sacrifices were burned on an altar. It was thought that the smoke was a pleasing smell to God. People sacrificed a portion of what they had in order to praise God and to show that they were willing to risk being dependent upon God's goodness to survive on what was left.

 TOGETHER

(1) Talk with your children about what you put in the offering plate. Tell them what amount you usually give, how you decided on that amount, and why you give anything at all. Generally, children learn about what they should give to the church as adults by observing their parents' actions. Do you put in a one-dollar bill every week? a full ten percent tithe? something in between? nothing?

(2) Next Sunday, let one of your children place the family's offering into the plate. Decide now who it will be. Afterwards, talk about how the child felt.

FAMILY FAITH BREAK

(1) Ask a family member to read aloud 1 Corinthians 16:1-3.

BIBLE HELP

Sometime during the middle of the first century, a serious famine struck the area around Jerusalem. Many of the early Christians were already poor. The famine would have affected them severely.

At several places in Paul's letters and in the Acts of the Apostles, a collection for the benefit of the Christians suffering from famine in Jerusalem is mentioned. Paul urged the Christians with whom he had contact throughout western Asia and southern Europe to give generously for hunger relief. Note that in 1 Corinthians 16:1-3, Paul suggests that the Christians in Corinth should do as he had also advised the Christians in Galatia: take up a collection for hunger relief every Sunday when they gather for worship.

(2) Just as you need to talk as a family about how much you do and should give in the offering each week, you also need to talk about how the offering is used. You will need a copy of the budget for your church in advance of this "Talk Together" time. (Your FaithHome leader will provide this for you.) What kinds of things appear in that budget? These are the things that your offering is used for. Most church budgets cover such things as

- paying the church's bills;
- keeping the church building in good repair;
- paying the salary of the church staff, including the pastor(s);
- paying "apportionments" for use in the connectional ministries of your church. These include paying for such things as the expenses of a denomination beyond your local church and for support of local and global mission outreach programs—for example, feeding the hungry, sharing Christian love with the suffering, and providing for the needs of the poor.

Explain that the leaders of your church have decided that these are the important things that the money given in the offering will be used to support. Therefore, whenever you place your gift in the offering plate, you help to pay the church's bills, keep the church building in good repair, make sure that a pastor and other members of the church staff are available to offer care and ministries, and make possible mission work and provisions to help poor persons.

(3) If your children do not already have the habit of giving an offering themselves during Sunday school or worship, talk with them about beginning this practice. In particular, if they receive an allowance or earn some money, discuss what would be an appropriate amount to give as an offering. You might want to read with them the story found in Luke 21:1-4. Talk as a family about what you think this Bible passage means for you.

Prayer:

Close with a prayer using your own words or using these words:

Dear God, help us remember that all we have, we have received from you. Help us to be generous in offering a portion back to you so that your gifts to us might help other persons. We pray in Jesus' name. Amen.

Day 4: We Are a Witnessing and Serving Church: Don't Hide Your Light

One pastor likes to offer this benediction at the close of each worship service: "This service of worship is over; your service to the world now begins."

For the past seven days, you have been talking about what takes place as you worship God as part of the church. Because we participate in corporate worship services inside the sanctuary within a church's building, we often think of participating in worship as "going to church." Some persons even think that simply "going to church" is enough to be a Christian.

Although worshiping God within the life of a local church is an important part of being a Christian, being a Christian involves more than "going to church." For the next several days, you will look at how the church is also a witnessing and serving community. This means that we reach out beyond ourselves to share with others what we find to be important about knowing God through Jesus Christ and to help those persons around us who have needs of various kinds.

 BACKGROUND BASICS

It has been said that God's kingdom, God's reign, is both here and hereafter—both "now" and "to come." In Luke's Gospel we read, "Once Jesus was asked by the Pharisees when the kingdom of God was coming, and he answered, 'The kingdom of God is not coming with things that can be observed; nor will they say, "Look, here it is!" or "There it is!" For, in fact, the kingdom of God is among you' " (17:20-21). When we reach out to others in Christian witness and service, we are helping to make God's kingdom a reality here on earth. God reigns *now!*

Jesus' own life and lifestyle demonstrated the very kingdom he announced. He lived life joyfully in obedience to God and in service to others. People experienced the new life of the Kingdom as they responded to the preaching, teaching, healing touch, and caring ministry of Jesus. Though we may grow in our understanding of the Kingdom, the kingdom of God has already been perfectly demonstrated in and through Jesus. We are merely given the responsibility of offering ourselves in ways that help to make known the Kingdom to the hurting, the helpless, and the marginalized.

Kingdom living has a particular focus on the poor, who are viewed, not as objects of mission, but as members of Jesus' family with whom we have a relationship, a relationship that includes responsibility. Unfortunately, in our affluent society it is not uncommon to hear Christians disparage the poor. It comes as a shock to success-oriented achievers to discover that the poor may have a better chance of "success" in being participants in the Kingdom than the affluent have. Jesus said, "For those who want to save their life will lose it, and those who lose their life for my sake, and for the sake of the gospel, will save it. For what will it profit them to gain the whole world and forfeit their life?" (Mark 8:35-36).

Kingdom living involves selfless giving. It involves all of who we are, including our wealth. Jesus said, "Where your treasure is, there your heart will be also" (Matthew 6:21). The biblical guideline for the giving of our income is a tithe—ten percent. Christians sometimes wonder whether the tithe is figured on one's "take home pay" or "gross income." Perhaps the best answer is that God is not interested in legalism. God wants us joyfully to share our resources on behalf of all God's children. The apostle Paul said it this way: "Each of you must give as you have made up your mind, not reluctantly or under compulsion, for God loves a cheerful giver" (2 Corinthians 9:7). When we teach our children to be selfless givers, we teach them how to live in God's kingdom.

Kingdom living also involves servanthood. Jesus took a basin and towel and washed the tired, dusty feet of his companions. Then he commanded them to imitate his example (see John 13:13-17). Serving God by serving others is the lifestyle of a Christian.

 ## TOGETHER

(1) Talk together as a family about the extent to which you think your neighbors (at least those living next door to you and across the way from you) know that you are Christians. If you wish, try this: Phone or visit one or more of your neighbors. Explain that you are working as a family on an experiment for a project at your church. Ask them if they already knew you were Christians and ask them how they knew (or why they did not know).

If you try this experiment, you might hear one of these responses:

- We see you going to church every Sunday morning.

- The cross you have on your dining room wall is a real giveaway!

- Of course! We go to the same church as you do!

- I think you once mentioned to me something that was going on at your church.

- You have always acted like a Christian towards me.

(2) Talk as a family about the extent you want to be known as Christians to the people you meet. For many older children, especially teenagers, being Christian is not always considered "cool." Discuss with sensitivity how it feels to be thought of as a Christian if persons around you joke about that or even insult you for it.

 FAMILY FAITH BREAK

(1) Ask a family member to read aloud Matthew 5:14-16.

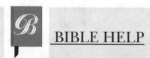 BIBLE HELP

In Matthew's Gospel, Chapters 5–7 contain the longest section of Jesus' recorded teachings. These chapters are often called the "Sermon on the Mount" because at the beginning of Chapter 5, we are told that Jesus "went up the mountain" where he began to speak and teach. Much of the Sermon on the Mount shows Jesus' concern that people obey the spirit of God's law more than the letter of that law.

After reading Matthew 5:14-16, read Chapters 5–7 as a whole to gain a larger understanding of Jesus' teachings about how Christians should live and behave.

(2) Try this experiment to appreciate the point of Matthew 5:14-16. You will need a candle, matches, candle holder, and a ceramic or metal container that is large enough to cover the candle.

Light the candle and place it in the candle holder, setting it in a safe place, preferably in a darkened room. What can family members say about the lighted candle? (It gives some light in the room. We can see it from X feet away. It's bright.)

Then cover the lighted candle with the container. Now what can family members say about the lighted candle? (We can't see it anymore. It doesn't do us any good now. If we leave it under there, it'll go out.)

After completing your experiment, talk about what you think Jesus is saying to you in Matthew 5:14-16.

(3) Sing the song "I Have Decided (to Follow Jesus)," "Jesus Is Calling," or "D-I-S-C-I-P-L-E-S" (all on the FaithHome cassette tape).

Prayer:

Close this time with a prayer using your own words or using these words:

Dear God, help us to be the kind of light that shows you to the world. We pray in Jesus' name. Amen.

Day 5: We Are a Witnessing and Serving Church: Sharing with Other Christians

"This is mine; that is yours!" "I want that one!" "He took my truck!" "She won't let me play with it!"

Sharing comes hard to children—and to adults. Most of us have been taught, to some extent, to value possessions. We buy. We get. We hang on to. We protect. We buy even more. We want to have the largest collection of baseball cards or the nicest bicycle or a better home or a lot more money. In fact, we often judge people by what they own. Are you more likely to want to become friends with someone who drives a nice new car or a ten-year-old, rusty, noisy car with chipping paint?

Many of the teachings of the Christian faith talk about sharing, but that is not the way the world normally works. We are our children's teachers. What are they learning? Do you know a child like the boy in this story?

> Ryan was the son of a financially successful medical professional. He and his family lived in an expensive, even elaborate, house on a large lot in a nice neighborhood on the edge of town, conveniently located to schools, stores, and anything else they might want. His family had two expensive cars. He never went hungry. He always had the clothes he (or his parents) wanted. He had plenty of things to amuse him.
>
> Ryan sat in his fifth-grade Sunday school class one Sunday in December. The Sunday school lesson was based on Luke 1:46-55—the Magnificat, which is the words Mary, the mother of Jesus, spoke after she became pregnant with Jesus and then met with her cousin, Elizabeth. When the Magnificat was read aloud and the class came to verse 53, the boy could not help exclaiming, "What? He has filled the hungry with good things, and sent the rich away empty?" The teacher explained that the verse evidently was saying that God took the side of the poor and needy. "But we're rich!" he said.

Obviously, the Bible passage bothered Ryan, who came from a well-off family. This was the first time he was challenged with the thought that owning a lot of possessions did not necessarily mean that he also had God's blessing.

 TOGETHER

(1) Talk about who owns what in your family. In some families, it is understood that the family owns everything and that the family provides what individual family members need. Sometimes this means that older sisters or brothers work after they receive their education in order to provide for the education of the younger sisters and brothers. In other families, some things belong to the family, and a few things belong to individuals. "That is our swing on the back deck, but that baseball glove belongs to my older brother!"

(2) Discuss whether everyone in your family gets what he or she needs. If someone needs something—if that something is really a matter of survival and not a luxury—is that something ever withheld if the family or someone within the family already possesses it or has the means to obtain it?

Usually, families look out for their members. Part of good parenting is making sure that children have what they need. Older children are often told that part of their responsibility is to make sure younger children are kept safe. When families work the way they are supposed to, the needs of all are met.

 FAMILY FAITH BREAK

(1) Ask a family member to read aloud Acts 4:32-35.

 BIBLE HELP

Acts 4:32-35 portrays the earliest community of Christians in Jerusalem as an ideal model of unity and sharing. Verse 32 implies a sort of "Christian communism." While the notion of giving up private ownership in order to share everything in common sounds alien to most of us, note how positively this passage depicts this model.

(2) Talk as a family about the ways your church resembles a family. Some ways that a church might resemble a family include these:

- Church members spend a lot of time talking to one another.
- Sometimes church members bicker among themselves.

- Church members share meals sometimes, such as potluck suppers.
- When someone is in great need, especially when there is some serious illness or injury, church people show they care through prayer and helping out.
- In some churches, members address one another as "Brother So-and-so" or "Sister This-or-that."

(3) Discuss: To what extent should you treat the people in your church as if they were members of your family? What would happen if you shared with them in the same ways you share what you have within your family?

(4) Talk about whether there is one new thing your family has that you might share with your church or with members of your church who are in need.

Prayer:

Close with a prayer using your own words or using these words:

Dear God, it is hard to share. Help us to be less selfish and to see the other members of our church as members of our family. In Jesus' name we pray. Amen.

Day 6: We Are a Witnessing and Serving Church: Sharing with Others Who Are Not Like Us

It is hard enough to share what we have with people within our family or within our church. Do we have to share also with those outside of our family and church? Shouldn't charity begin at home? What if there isn't enough to go around? And are we really supposed to help "them" out?

Just as God's love knows no limits, so also God expects our love for those around us to become limitless. But among the things constricting our love for others are our prejudices. Often, the prejudices we carry are those we learned from our parents. And just as often, the breaking down of prejudice begins with a lesson we learned from our parents.

A white man who is now in his forties recalls growing up during the 1950s in Washington, D.C., in the house his parents shared with his mother's grandmother. Granny was often upset because families from other ethnic backgrounds were moving into the neighborhood. In fact, one such family was now living next door. Granny often used a racial epitaph when talking about the family next door.

The man remembers one time when he was a small boy in the back yard with his parents. He used the word he had heard Granny use on occasion. He remembers his parents were appalled and as angry with him as they had ever been.

"Don't you ever use that word again! That is a bad word!" they told him.

"But Granny calls them that!" he replied.

"Granny is wrong to use that word. They are good people. We should treat them with respect," his parents explained.

Treating persons of a different color, of a different race, with respect is a lesson this man learned from his parents and one he has tried to apply to his daily life ever since.

 TOGETHER

(1) Before you talk with your family today, think about the prejudices you might have concerning people who are not like you. (Couples should discuss this together.) Today it almost seems fashionable to joke about "political correctness." However, how we treat persons who are different from us, especially those who might have a less-privileged place within our society, is a serious matter before God. It is also serious because your children will learn how they should relate to persons who are different from them based on what they see in your behavior.

(2) Because children tend to think concretely, talk about particular persons they know rather than about an abstract category of people, such as an ethnic group or a religious group. Ask your children about friends or classmates at school who are of a different race, nationality, or religion. Talk about:

- How are they different from you?
- How are they like you?

- What do you think of them?
- What do you like about them?
- What do you not like about them?
- Would you call them friends of yours?
- Do you know other people who give them a hard time? If so, what happens? What do you do when that happens?
- Do you ever treat them badly?
- Is there anything that you should change about the way you treat them?

 ## FAMILY FAITH BREAK

(1) Ask a family member to read aloud Luke 10:25-37.

 ## BIBLE HELP

Luke 10:25-37 sets up and tells the parable of the good Samaritan. Jesus often taught using parables, which are brief stories that seek to make some point, usually about what the kingdom of God is like, and that use experiences and things from the everyday lives of the persons to whom Jesus was speaking. The parable of the good Samaritan is one of the most popular and familiar of the parables. In Jesus' time, persons would have known about the things Jesus alluded to; and yet they would have been surprised by the twist he gave to the story.

Jesus told the story to answer the question, "And who is my neighbor?" His first hearers would have readily known that the road through the hills between Jerusalem and Jericho often held dangerous highway robbers. Also, as Jews, they would have held a deep-seated prejudice against Samaritans. Samaritans were considered "half-breeds," being the products of centuries of intermarriage between the northern Jews of the former Kingdom of Israel and the surrounding non-Jewish peoples. Samaritans were considered blasphemers or heretics, although they claimed to worship the same God that the Jews did. Jews brought all their sacrifices to the Temple in Jerusalem. Samaritans worshiped God at shrines in the hill country of Samaria. Jews would not have expected Samaritans to treat the injured Jew with mercy, hospitality, kindness, or generosity.

The "punchline" is found in verses 36 and 37. Jesus told the lawyer and his other listeners that if they wanted to do God's will, they should behave just like the Samaritan in the story.

(2) As a family, work together to write a modern paraphrase of the parable of the good Samaritan (Luke 10:29-37). Update the parable so

that it addresses situations and prejudices within your own community or experience. Even if your children are not yet able to read, they can listen to the original Bible story and suggest ways to tell the same story as if it happened today.

Prayer:

Close your time with a prayer using your own words or using these words:

Dear God, help us to love other people even as much as we love ourselves or members of our own family. In Jesus' name we pray. Amen.

Day 7: We Are a Witnessing and Serving Church: Justice

Philosophers and political theorists often define the word *justice* as giving to each person that which is due to him or her. We may accept that definition; but the key issue will always be, How do we determine what is due to persons?

After reading the teachings of Jesus in the New Testament and those of the prophets in the Old Testament, there can be no doubt that one of God's priorities is that there be justice on earth.

talk TOGETHER

"That's not fair! He got to ride up the street on his bike and I didn't. I had to stay in the driveway."

Children become interested in matters of justice at an early age, especially when justice and fairness are seen as means to get their own way. It does not matter to a young child that he is five years old while his brother—who got to ride his bicycle all the way up the street—is eleven. From this one, small example, we can see two problems with the way we often think about justice:

- Justice does not mean that all people are treated exactly the same. Sometimes different circumstances require different treatment in the name of justice.

- Justice does not mean that you always will, or should, get your own way.

Older children especially think in terms of a legal definition of justice. If you play by the rules, then X should always happen because the rules say so. And if you break the rules, then Y should always happen, again because the rules say so.

(1) Talk with your children about how they understand justice or fairness. Ask them to describe a time when they saw someone else being treated unfairly or unjustly. What made the treatment unfair or unjust? What happened as a result? How did they feel about it? What did they do about it?

(2) Explain the two problems with the way we often think about justice and ask family members if they can think of examples of each. (Provide examples for young children.)

 ## FAMILY FAITH BREAK

(1) Ask a family member to read aloud Micah 6:6-8.

 ## BIBLE HELP

The prophet Micah came from a small town in the hills to the southwest of the capital city of Jerusalem. He lived in Judah during the eighth century before Christ, which was a time marked by the contrasts of apparent prosperity and peace yet underlying economic corruption and political stupidity. Assyria was the dominant world power of the time, conquering the northern Kingdom of Israel and rendering the southern Kingdom of Judah into a vassal state.

Among other things, Micah prophesied that because Judah's rulers were so corrupt, Jerusalem and the Temple would be destroyed. Though Micah 6:6-8 is perhaps the most famous portion of this book, read also Chapter 3 to get a feel for the social and political problems Micah condemned.

In Micah 6:6-8, the prophet is describing what God desires and requires of us.

(2) Explain that in the Bible, justice usually means making sure that the weakest persons receive their due. Stronger persons are able, through force, to ensure they get what is due to them, and sometimes, unjustly, more than their due. Weaker persons sometimes have to have someone take their side. According to the prophets and to Jesus, God takes the side of the weaker persons. Talk about what this means, both for relationships within your family as well as for the dealings your family has with others.

For example, justice might require that an older brother help protect the interests of a younger brother when they are together playing with neighborhood children, some of whom might be bullies. Or in many families, when two siblings are sharing a piece of cake, one cuts it while the other gets to choose a piece first. Or maybe at school, children may need to take up for someone who is being picked on and certainly will need to make sure that they themselves are not doing the oppressing. What other examples of justice can family members think of?

Prayer:

Close with a prayer using your own words or using these words:

Dear God, help us to love justice as much as you do; and help us to treat people justly. In Jesus' name we pray. Amen.

 ## FAMILY MEALS

Family Meal #1

- Weather allowing, "fire up the grill"! Select some of the foods you most enjoy. If it is too cool outside for grilling, make "Supper on a Stick" over a small indoor grill or under your oven's broiler.

Supper on a Stick

Ingredients: enough meat to feed your family (stew meat, hot dogs, or chicken)
vegetables such as onions, cherry tomatoes, potatoes, green peppers, zucchini, and mushrooms
pineapple chunks

Directions:

Cut meat and vegetables into small cubes. Drain pineapple chunks. Skewer the meat, vegetables, and pineapple on metal or wooden skewers, alternating the ingredients. Grill to desired "doneness."

- Make dinner preparation a fun event! Create an "assembly line" and let the whole family help to fill the skewers. One person might be responsible for adding the green pepper, another for the meat, and so forth. If things begin to get a bit complicated, just "back off" and simplify. After all, the goal is not perfect cuisine but family memories and bonding!

- Complete your meal with warm rolls or bread, a salad, and dessert if you wish.

- Light the Christ candle at the beginning of your meal and invite a family member who does not often pray aloud to lead grace. Or, vary your regular mealtime prayer in another way—with song. Sing together "Praise God, from Whom All Blessings Flow" or another musical blessing.

Conversation Starters:

- Talk about the fun you have had preparing this meal!

- Draw upon the "Talk Together" suggestions for this day, or make your daily "Family Faith Break" part of your mealtime together.

- Take a peek at this week's "Reaching Beyond the Family" activity. When can you do it? Also plan when you will have your next family meal.

Family Meal #2

Did you know that there is a national restaurant chain that offers "comfort foods" such as meatloaf and mashed potatoes to over-stressed business executives in need of some comfort? Apparently, the idea has caught on. The restaurant chain is doing well! Perhaps the owners had a firm grasp of the obvious: Food is used as much for comfort as for nutrition.

- Who is most in need of comfort in your family this week? Sometimes when we are feeling discouraged, it helps to know that there is a comforting, delicious meal awaiting us at home. If someone in your family is going through a difficult time, ask him or her, "What would you like to eat for supper?" Plan the menu around him or her. Or, invite each member of your family to request one part of the meal, such as a dessert or vegetable. It does not need to be fancy. It will be full of love!

- Light the Christ candle at the beginning of your meal and say a prayer, such as this one:

Thank you, God, for the many ways you provide our family with comfort. Bless our meal and the hands that prepared it. Amen.

Conversation Starters:

- Plan to have your "Talk Together" time and "Family Faith Break" at another time. During this family meal, share your love and concern for one another, especially for a member of your family who may need comforting. Talk about favorite family memories and fun times. Tell jokes. Laugh. Make it a special time you will not soon forget!

- Plan when you will have your next family meal.

 ## REACHING BEYOND THE FAMILY

Review the "Reaching Beyond the Family" ideas for the last several weeks. More has been suggested than most families will have been able to do. This week, choose to reach beyond your family using one of the suggestions from an earlier week. For example, perhaps you planted a tree early in your FaithHome experience, when you were focusing on God the Creator. Perhaps now you would like to reorganize—or begin for the first time—your family recycling efforts.

Simply review past suggestions and choose what form of outreach you will do this week. Record below how you reached beyond your family— and why. You might even have enough space to mount a family photograph of your efforts!

Day 1: We Are a Witnessing and Serving Church: Peace

Today you will consider how we are called to be peacemakers in the world.

 TOGETHER

(1) As a family, try to remember as much as you can about your separate group experiences during the FaithHome session and talk about them together.

(2) Invite each member of the family to share one thing that he or she heard during the session that was new or important to him or her.

(3) You are now beginning your seventh week of FaithHome. Take the time to talk as a family about your experience:

- What is the most important thing that has happened to your family during the past week?
- How do you think God was involved with your family during that "most important thing"?
- What difference has FaithHome made so far in the ways your family thinks about God?

(4) If your children are of the age when they are interested in watching cartoons, sit down and watch thirty minutes or so of cartoons with them. Or if your children have outgrown cartoons, watch a prime time television program other than a comedy for thirty minutes or so. Watch for the occasions in the cartoon or the program when someone uses violence. You may be surprised at how violent some cartoons and prime time programs really are.

Talk with your children about the violence. Ask them:

- What did you think about (name the violence you saw)?
- How did you feel about it?
- What we've just seen on TV was "make believe," but how would you feel about it if it were real?

- What ways might there be to handle a situation other than by violence?

 ## FAMILY FAITH BREAK

(1) Ask a family member to read aloud Matthew 5:9, 38-48.

 ## BIBLE HELP

A few days ago you were introduced to the fifth chapter of Matthew's Gospel and Jesus' Sermon on the Mount. Today's first portion of Scripture, verse 9, is from a section of the Sermon on the Mount often called the Beatitudes. *Beatitude* is another word for "blessing." You can see that in verses 3-11, Jesus pronounces various blessings on persons who have sought to live according to God's will. The blessing in verse 9 is for those persons who have worked to make peace. Note that it does not say, "Blessed are the peaceful" or "the peaceable." Rather, it says, "the peacemakers."

Verses 38-48 appear to spell out some ways to work to make peace— ways that seem to go against common sense. Evidently, we are supposed to refuse to hit back when someone hits us and to show love for those enemies who seek to do us harm. What would happen if we actually tried to live this way? Wouldn't it be dangerous? Perhaps. But it also would be Christian.

Verses 9 and 48 convey the same important truth: When you act in such a way as to make peace, you are acting in a way that is perfect, just as God is perfect. Those who do so are "children of God"; they act in a way that is so much like God that God claims them as God's own. God's own character is one that seeks to make peace.

(2) One of the best ways to avoid resorting to violence is to think in advance of what you might do instead. Talk with your children about what they can do in difficult situations such as when a bully threatens them with violence or otherwise picks on them. Alternatives to violence might include

- running away (Most police officers advise that when someone wants to do you harm, you are better off trying to escape right away rather than doing what the person wants or fighting back.);

- talking your way out of the situation;
- telling someone in authority, such as a parent, a teacher, or a police officer;
- avoiding situations that might prove dangerous, as much as possible.

Certainly, you do not want your children to be harmed in any way. No parent does. The temptation is to teach them to "take care of themselves." However, as Christians we must recognize that our children can be harmed spiritually by resorting to violence in ways that may be worse than suffering physical violence. And resorting to violence never guarantees that the justified party will emerge victorious from a fight.

Talking about peaceful alternatives to violence may be one of those conversations that needs to continue for many days. And remember, children are more likely to do as they see you do.

Prayer:

Offer a prayer using your own words or using these words:

Dear God, help us to be strong, brave, and peaceful, even when those around us are not. Be with us and deliver us from the evil that threatens us. In Jesus' name we pray. Amen.

Day 2: We Are a Witnessing and Serving Church: Charity (Love)

We have mixed feelings when we hear the word *charity* today. When we give money or goods for charity, we hope our gift will benefit someone who really needs help rather than someone who is shirking from work or responsibility. And when we give money or goods for charity, we tend to give only that which is left over. We give our extra stuff, or sometimes even our damaged goods. We take care of our own needs and some of our own luxuries before we give for charity.

These modern-day dynamics have nothing to do with the first meaning of the word *charity*. Originally, charity meant love—in Latin, the word was *caritas*—the kind of unreserved love of which God is capable and which we are called to imitate. Charitable giving is meant to be what we give to persons in need because we love them as God loves them.

 ## TOGETHER

(1) What charitable gifts has your family given recently? To whom? What motivated you to make this gift of money or goods?

(2) Talk together as a family about a homeless person you have seen in your area recently. If you live in or near an urban area, you might see homeless persons regularly. Often they can be seen standing on the street corner or by an expressway exit ramp, holding a sign and hoping for money or food. Sometimes they might be found carrying a pack or a bag or pushing an old shopping cart. During colder weather, homeless persons might be found sleeping at night over a grate that releases hot exhaust air from a skyscraper. They are indeed a reminder that the poor are always with us.

Even if you live in a small town or in a rural area, the poor are with you. Maybe an older adult lives in a house that is really a hut on the edge of town. Maybe migrating workers get on and off boxcars at the railroad crossing near your home. Maybe someone sleeps on occasion underneath a bridge where the interstate crosses a dirt road a mile or two from your farm.

Discuss:

- What did you think and feel when you saw this person?
- Did you do or say anything?
- Did you have any idea about what this person's story might be?
- Did you think about offering charity to this person? Why or why not?

 ## FAMILY FAITH BREAK

(1) Ask a family member to read aloud Matthew 25:31-40.

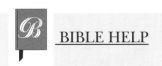

BIBLE HELP

The passage you are looking at today is a portion of Jesus' teaching about the Last Judgment. Jesus is saying that the people of the world will be judged by him on the basis of whether they help those persons around them who are in some kind of need. Those who help the most insignificant needy person are helping Jesus himself and are deemed worthy to inherit the kingdom of God.

The examples Jesus gives of how his followers will help the needy include

- giving food to the hungry
- giving something to drink to the thirsty
- welcoming the stranger
- giving clothing to persons without clothing
- taking care of persons who are sick
- visiting prisoners

This teaching about the Last Judgment continues after verse 40. In Matthew 25:41-46, Jesus says that those who neglect to help needy persons have actually rejected him and will find themselves condemned to eternal punishment. For most of us, this is a scary thought when we realize how little we have done and how much we have left undone.

(2) Talk together about the ways you have or have not offered help to persons in need in the six specific ways that Jesus named in Matthew 25:35-36. Think about ways that you might do each of these things as a family *on an ongoing basis.*

Too often, we do one or more of these six things once and think that is enough. For example, someone might give the clothing left over after a garage sale to a nearby shelter for homeless persons. That is well and good, but what might be done on an ongoing basis?

Many people today want to keep persons in need at arm's length. They think it is all right to give something to an agency that will see that their items get to the needy, but they do not want to meet those needy people in person.

Coming face-to-face with persons in need can be uncomfortable. And yet those who personally care for the needs of others have been told by Jesus that they are really caring for Jesus himself.

Determine ways your family can begin to help persons in need on an ongoing basis.

Prayer:

Close this time with a prayer using your own words or using these words:

Dear God, help us to feel love for the persons around us who are in need. Help us to transform our love into the kind of true charity that seeks to help because of love. In Jesus' name we pray. Amen.

Day 3: We Are a Witnessing and Serving Church: Hospitality

Genesis 18:1-8 tells a wonderful story about hospitality. One hot summer's day, Abraham was sitting at the entrance of his tent, trying to catch a cool breeze. All of a sudden, he noticed three men standing nearby. Although Abraham did not know it at the time, the three men were really a manifestation of God. Abraham jumped to his feet; ran to meet them; and bowed low to the ground, saying, "Please have a seat in the shade. Let me bring to you some water to wash and cool your feet, and let me bring a little bread so that you don't leave hungry." Abraham had nothing to gain by making such an offer; he simply wanted to be hospitable to strangers passing by.

Note what happened next. Abraham ran into the tent and gave directions to Sarah and the servants to prepare a feast for the strangers. When he brought the meal to them, it included cakes made from choice flour, veal cutlets, curds, and milk. Then he hovered nearby to see if they needed anything else.

This is a model for hospitality offered to strangers in the expectation of nothing in return. What kind of hospitality do we offer as Christians to strangers today?

 TOGETHER

(1) Talk about the last time your family extended hospitality to someone in your home. What did you do to make your guest feel welcome and comfortable? Did it require any extra effort on your part? Did you receive anything in return?

(2) Think as a family of a time in the not-too-distant past when *you* felt truly welcome somewhere you went. Maybe it was at a restaurant, a hotel, a church, or even a friend's house. Talk about

- What in particular made you feel welcome?
- Did the welcome you received require any effort on the part of your host?
- Did your host receive anything in return from you?
- Did you learn anything about how to make someone feel welcome?

 FAMILY FAITH BREAK

(1) Ask a family member to read aloud Hebrews 13:2.

 BIBLE HELP

The passage you are looking at today comes towards the end of a long letter that seeks to help some long-suffering Jewish Christians remain strong in their faith. The verse you are reading is within a section presenting several admonitions and pieces of advice for Christian living.

Reading between the lines, one might wonder whether some of the early Christians begrudged sharing what they had with strangers as they made the effort to show Christian hospitality. First Peter 4:9 gives similar advice in slightly different words: "Be hospitable to one another without complaining."

Do not get hung up on the mention of "angels" in Hebrews 13:2. "Angels" refers to the strangers who were offered hospitality by Abraham, according to Genesis 18. Literally, an "angel" is a "messenger of God." Sometimes those we serve through hospitality might give us some glimpse of what God wills for us.

(2) What can your family do to practice the virtue of hospitality? You might make plans about what you would do if a stranger did in fact come to your door. How would you make her or him feel welcome in your home?

Or maybe you could make plans for how you would welcome someone who has come to a worship service or fellowship event at your church for the first time. How might you make that person feel welcome?

Or, to gain some practice in hospitality, plan for each member of your family to take a turn offering hospitality to the other members of the family one evening this week. What might you do to take the worries and cares of everyday life off of one of your family members for a few hours during an evening? Practice in offering hospitality to family members can be helpful when an occasion for offering hospitality to a stranger presents itself.

Prayer:

Close this time by offering a prayer using your own words or using these words:

Dear God, help us to be generous in offering our hospitality to those around us. In Jesus' name we pray. Amen.

Day 4: Living with the Bible: Scripture

A young pastor was visiting with a family from church. The parents in the family obviously wanted to impress him. They made sure that he saw the large, new Bible placed conspicuously on the coffee table in the living room. The mother wanted to know something, however. "What can you tell me about this kind of Bible? I've seen this kind of Bible and that kind of Bible and other kinds of Bibles, but all I really want is a Holy Bible!" She was bothered by the fact that the front cover and the spine of the Bible were not imprinted with the words *Holy Bible.*

All versions of the Bible are holy Bibles! *Holy* is an adjective meaning that this is something that is sacred, set apart from the ordinary things of everyday life. To say that the Bible is holy means that it is different from all other books. Indeed it is, because it tells us about God better than any other book ever has!

Today we turn our focus to the Bible, which not only tells us about God but also teaches us how to live our lives.

 ## BACKGROUND BASICS

Every parent knows that children love stories, particularly stories that involve them or people they know. Parents often tell and retell stories about a child's birth, infancy, and young childhood. Stories help us to form our families and remind us of family history. Stories have power!

For Christians, there is great power in a particular story, the story of our faith. It is the story of a loving Creator God yearning for us, told throughout the pages of the Bible. The story begins with the creation of all that is and continues on to the covenant promises made to Israel, to the fulfillment of those promises in Jesus, and on to the promised culmination of Jesus' risen life in the kingdom of God.

The Bible is a book for all ages. We can be nourished from it throughout all our life. The act of sharing the Bible with our families sends a clear message about the importance of grounding our lives in God and in God's Word.

God, our loving Parent, is constantly seeking to nourish and renew a relationship with us. Regular personal and family Bible reading enables us to experience God's searching, welcoming love.

 ## TOGETHER

(1) Take five or ten minutes for your family to go on a "Bible hunt." Each member of the family should go looking through your home to retrieve any Bible he or she can find. The youngest member of your family gets to "find" the Bible that you have been reading from each day during your "Family Faith Break."

(2) When all the Bibles have been collected, take some time to look through them together. Become more familiar with what is in the Bible than you already are—where certain books are found, how to find specific chapters and verses, and so forth.

Now look at what version or versions of the Bible you have. If you have an old "family Bible" that has been passed along from one generation to the next, it will probably be a King James Version, which was first published in 1611. Other versions include the New Revised Standard Version, the New International Version, the *Good News Bible: The Bible in Today's English Version*, the Contemporary English Version, the *New English Bible*, the Living Bible, and many more. Some families might even have a Bible in a language other than English.

Whatever version of the Bible helps you and your family get into the habit of reading it regularly is the best version for you. All the Bible versions have been translated by scholars from the Hebrew and Greek languages in which the books of the Bible were originally written.

(3) The word *Bible* literally means "book." Some people also call it "the Scripture" or "the Scriptures." *Scripture* is a word that means "writing." Can your family think of any other names by which people call the Bible?

 ## FAMILY FAITH BREAK

(1) Ask a family member to read aloud 2 Timothy 3:14-17.

 ## BIBLE HELP

Second Timothy is a letter filled with advice from an older missionary to a younger colleague. Perhaps the main message is a call to Timothy to stand firm in the same faith that he learned from his mother and grandmother while he was yet a child.

The "scripture" to which this Second Letter of Timothy refers is obviously what we today would call the Old Testament. The New Testament, of which Second Timothy is a part, had not yet been collected. Probably, all of the books that now make up the New Testament had not been written at this time.

To say that "all scripture is inspired by God" is to say that Christians believe God has "breathed" life into these particular writings. Some Christians believe that God dictated or compelled the writers of the Bible to write these particular words, at least as they appeared in the original manuscripts, none of which we have access to today. Other Christians are content to say that the Bible is inspired by God in that the writers are witnessing to their particular encounters with the living God. The words might still be human words, but the testimony is to God and to God's will for human beings.

Note also how verse 16 claims that the main purposes of Scripture have to do with teaching and training. We learn what to believe and what to do from the words of the Bible.

(2) Before the words of the Bible were ever written down, there were oral teachings and stories. Generations of Jews and later Christians shared with one another the important messages and accounts of events that taught them about God.

Take turns within your family so that each family member can tell about his or her favorite story, teaching, or verse from the Bible. (Younger children might have a favorite Bible song they would like to sing—perhaps one of the songs on your FaithHome tape.) Do not worry about remembering the story or teaching it exactly the way it appears in the Bible. Tell it the way you remember it. If you get stuck, let the other members of your family help you in the telling. Tell also why you like that story or passage. What makes it important for you?

In the space below, list each family member's favorite Bible story, teaching, or verse and why it is important to him or her:

Prayer:

Close with a prayer using your own words or using these words:

Dear God, thank you for letting us know you through the words of the Bible. In Jesus' name we pray. Amen.

Day 5: Living with the Bible: In Order That You Might Believe

How do you get to the point of being able to believe in God? Maybe for you or for your children, this is not a big question. Maybe you already have a deep and solid faith in a God who loves you and has made it possible through Jesus Christ for you to enjoy the fullness of life God intends you to enjoy eternally. But not everyone who is a Christian finds it easy to believe, at least not at first.

 TOGETHER

(1) If you have time, read aloud John 20:19-29, the passage that comes immediately before the "Family Faith Break" reading for today. Otherwise, summarize the story as it appears below:

> **This is the story of how the apostle Thomas came to believe that God had raised Thomas' friend and master, Jesus, from the dead. Today, we often call this the story of "Doubting Thomas." Thomas did indeed doubt at first that Jesus was alive again. Like many of us today, Thomas wanted proof. He wanted to be able to touch the wounds that caused Jesus' death before he would believe that Jesus was alive again. Jesus came to Thomas with exactly that proof. Jesus wanted Thomas to believe, and finally Thomas did believe. "My Lord and my God!" Thomas exclaimed. And Jesus responded, "Have you believed because you have seen me? Blessed are those who have not seen and yet have come to believe."**
>
> **Perhaps we really should call Thomas "Believing Thomas."**

(2) Talk as a family about what it takes, or what it would take, for each one of you to believe in God. Before you start sharing, make sure that everyone knows that wherever any of you happen to be in your struggle to believe is OK. And make sure family members know that whatever

they share during this time is accepted as part of their story. There are no right or wrong responses at this time—only the possibility for openness, truth, and growth in faith.

 ## FAMILY FAITH BREAK

(1) Ask a family member to read aloud John 20:30-31.

 ## BIBLE HELP

This passage is the "punchline" to the Gospel of John. It tells why John wrote down his remembrances of and reflections on the teachings and events from the life of Jesus. Many Bible scholars think that this Gospel was written by one of Jesus' original disciples, perhaps "the disciple whom Jesus loved," now writing as an old man living in the city of Ephesus.

John's purpose for writing this book is "so that you may come to believe that Jesus is the Messiah, the Son of God, and that through believing you may have life in his name" (20:31). (*Messiah* is the Hebrew word for *Christ*, which is a Greek word meaning "the anointed one." The Messiah is the one anointed, set apart, and sent by God.) Everything John has included in this book is for this single purpose—that you might believe and come to have the life God wants you to have. This book of the Bible, at least, is intended to persuade you; to convince you; to prove to you the truth about God's love for you shown in the life, death, and resurrection of Jesus Christ.

(2) You have read many passages from the Bible as part of your daily FaithHome experience. See how many of these passages your family can recall. Name as many as you can—by book, chapter, and verse or by theme, story, or main point. Talk about how some or all of these passages have helped any of you to believe in God:

- What have they taught you?
- How have they helped you know how to live?
- What changes, large or small, have any of you made because of what you have read in the Bible during these FaithHome times?

Prayer:

Close this time with a prayer using your own words or using these words:

Dear God, help us to find greater belief in you. Thank you for helping us learn about you in the words of the Bible. In Jesus' name we pray. Amen.

Day 6: Living with the Bible: Helping to Understand

 **TOGETHER**

(1) You will need a long piece of string (ten or fifteen feet). Find an uncluttered area in your home that is as long as your piece of string. Stretch the string out and lay it in a straight line on the floor in this area. Point to one end of the string and say:

This end is the number one.

Point to the other end and say:

This end is the number ten.

Continue by saying:

Think about all the Bible passages we have read during these past weeks of FaithHome. Think about how difficult or easy it has been to understand these Bible passages. On a scale from one to ten, with one being the lowest and ten being the highest, how well have you understood these Bible passages? Find a place along the string on the floor that corresponds with the number you chose.

Take note of where each family member stands along the string. How well are family members saying they understand the Bible passages? Talk together about the following questions:

- What parts of the Bible do you find easy to understand?
- What parts of the Bible do you find difficult to understand?
- What do you think makes those parts of the Bible difficult for you to understand?

For younger children:

Ask young children if they have learned a little, more than a little, or a lot about God, Jesus, and the Bible over the past several weeks. If possible, let an older brother or sister help them find their place on the string. Ask:

- What do you like about the Bible?
- What do you not like?
- Is there a saying or story that we've read from the Bible that you really like? Why?
- Is there a saying or story that we've read from the Bible that you really do not like? Why?

(2) Ask every family member to respond to these questions:

- If you could ask any question about the Bible or about a particular Bible passage, what would it be?
- Why would you ask that particular question?

 ## FAMILY FAITH BREAK

(1) Ask a family member to read aloud Acts 8:26-39.

 ## BIBLE HELP

The Book of the Acts of the Apostles tells the story of the spread of Christianity from its beginnings in a room in Jerusalem—with the gift of the Holy Spirit to the gathered disciples—into the rest of Judea, and from there to Samaria, throughout Palestine, into Asia Minor, and over into Europe to the capital of the Roman Empire itself.

Today's passage, from Acts 8:26-39, tells of the coming of faith to an Ethiopian. He was a highly regarded official in the court of the queen of Ethiopia. We might think of him as the secretary of the treasury. (You do not need to know the following details in order to understand the story, but you might be curious: [1] A eunuch was a man who was castrated in order to serve in the court of the queen. We might find such a practice abhorrent, but it was commonplace at that time and place. [2] "Candace" was not a name; it was a title meaning roughly the same thing as "queen.")

Apparently, the Ethiopian official was already sympathetic to the Jewish religion. He was returning home after spending some time in Jerusalem worshiping God at the Temple. He was reading from the Jewish Scriptures, the same writings Christians today call the Old Testament. When the apostle Philip happened upon him, the Ethiopian official was trying to figure out what Isaiah 53:7-8 was about. Philip explained that Christians understood that passage to be describing Jesus. After hearing Philip explain who Jesus was and what Jesus meant, the Ethiopian official insisted that Philip baptize him by the side of the road.

(2) Talk as a family about what you can do if one or more members of your family do not understand a particular passage in the Bible. Some ideas include

- talking about the passage as a family so that everyone is working at trying to understand it;
- obtaining a Bible with study notes (such as the *New Oxford Annotated Bible*);
- looking up information in reference tools such as a Bible dictionary, a Bible atlas, a concordance, or a commentary (Many churches have their own libraries with these kinds of Bible reference tools.);
- studying the Bible in Sunday school classes and other Bible study settings (such as *Disciple* Bible Study);
- asking your pastor specific questions.

Prayer:

Close this time with a prayer using your own words or using these words:

Dear God, sometimes we find it hard to understand what parts of the Bible mean. Thank you for sending us people like Philip to help us. In Jesus' name we pray. Amen.

Day 7:
Living with the Bible:
Sweeter Than Honey

TOGETHER

(1) Some time ago you studied Psalm 119—the longest psalm in the Bible. Remember how you searched to find all the words used to mean "God's law"? Take several minutes to read Psalm 119 again. This time, look for the benefits that this psalm says come to those who study and love God's law. For example, verse 9 claims that God's Word will help young people keep their lives pure—that is, without sin. Likewise, the best known of this psalm's verses, verse 105, states,

**Your word is a lamp to my feet
and a light to my path,**

implying that God's Word will guide your way through life.

(2) Write the benefits you find in the space below:

 FAMILY FAITH BREAK

(1) Ask a family member to read aloud Psalm 119:103.

 BIBLE HELP

See the "Bible Help" related to Psalm 119 on page 90.

(2) You will need several pieces of honeycomb or a jar of honey and several small spoons. Work as a family to help each member memorize Psalm 119:103:

**How sweet are your words to my taste,
sweeter than honey to my mouth!**

When a family member has recited this verse from memory (Young children can repeat the verse.), he or she can taste a piece of honeycomb or a small spoonful of honey. (If a family member is allergic to honey, provide some other treat.)

A Jewish custom that continues in synagogue school today uses honey to teach the sweetness of God's Word. As children succeed at learning the Hebrew language, which they use to read their Scriptures in the original language, a parent will place a piece of honeycomb or a bit of honey on the child's tongue. Not only does the sweet treat serve as a positive reinforcement for learning; it also makes the point through the sense of taste that God's Word itself is sweet.

Prayer:

Close this time with a prayer in your own words, or say together Psalm 119:103.

Dear God, "How sweet are your words to my taste,/sweeter than honey to my mouth!" In Jesus' name we pray. Amen.

FAMILY MEALS

Family Meal #1

- Have a theme meal! Choose the nationality (Asian, Italian, French, and so forth) and create an "international" flavor for your family meal—or visit a restaurant that specializes in this kind of food.

- Young readers might enjoy researching the nation whose food you are eating. Encourage them to share some of their findings at the table.

- Decorate the table with maps, pictures, artifacts, and other items from that country.

- If your family enjoys ethnic meals, you might want to feature a dessert, salad, or main dish from a different country several nights in a row! Decorate your table to reflect the different cultures or nations featured.

- Light the Christ candle and place it in the center of your table amid the decorations as a visible reminder that Christ came to all people of the world.

• Say a prayer, such as this one:

Dear God, thank you for sending your Son for all the world. We celebrate the different peoples of the world and our own unique family. Bless this meal and those gathered around this table. In Jesus' name. Amen.

Conversation Starters:

• Talk about the "host nation" of your theme meal. Why did you choose this country? What did family members learn about it while preparing for the meal? What do you find interesting about the country and its customs? What foods from this country do you particularly like or dislike?

• Talk about the many different peoples and cultures of our world. Can family members think of ways we all are alike? You might ask:

Do you think we're all children of God? Why or why not?

• Draw upon the "Talk Together" suggestions for this day or make your daily "Family Faith Break" part of your mealtime together.

• Plan when you will have your next family meal, as well as this week's "Reaching Beyond the Family" activity.

Family Meal #2

• Celebrate family togetherness with a fun twist on a favorite family fare: cheeseburgers!

Family-Size Open-Face Cheeseburger

Ingredients: 2 cups baking mix
(such as Bisquick)
1/2 cup milk
1 pound ground beef
1/4 cup chopped onion
1 cup ketchup
1 teaspoon dry mustard
1/8 teaspoon pepper
6 slices process American cheese (3 1/2 inch square each)

Directions:

Heat oven to 450 degrees. Grease a cookie sheet. Mix baking mix and milk until soft dough forms. Beat vigorously 30 seconds. Turn onto surface, well dusted with baking mix; roll gently in baking mix to coat. Knead 10 times. Pat or roll dough into 12" x 8" rectangle on cookie sheet. Bake until light brown and puffed, about 8 minutes.

Cook and stir ground beef and onion in 10" skillet over medium heat until meat is brown; drain thoroughly. Stir in ketchup, dry mustard, and pepper. Spread over hot crust. Bake until beef mixture is hot, 8-10 minutes. Top with cheese; bake until cheese is melted, 1-2 minutes longer. (Serves 6)[1]

- Add a salad and fruit for a quick, nutritious meal.

- Children may enjoy helping to prepare this family-sized burger. Even young children can help to knead and roll dough!

- Light the Christ candle and say a prayer, such as this one:

Dear God, once again we bow our heads and thank you for the gifts of food and family. Amen.

Conversation Starters:

- Draw upon the "Talk Together" suggestions for this day or make your daily "Family Faith Break" part of your mealtime together.

- Plan when you will have your next family meal.

 ## REACHING BEYOND THE FAMILY

During the week you have focused on the power of the Story—the Scriptures. Consider one of the following activities for your family outreach project this week:

Option A:

Experience the joy of sharing the biblical story with a group of children. Volunteer as substitutes—or "extra hands"—in a children's classroom of your local church. Your pastor or professional staff educator will be pleased to use your abilities and can be helpful to you in preparing materials or lessons for your chosen age group.

Option B:

So often we think that the Bible is readily available to everyone, yet there are still many people throughout the world—including many in our own communities—who have not been introduced to the Scriptures. Ask your pastor if there is a need for more Bibles in your church or if there is a community organization or group in need of Bibles; then donate one or more!

Day 1: Living with the Bible: Scripture Fulfilled

The word *gospel* literally means "good news." The Scriptures of the Old Testament and New Testament, as they point to Jesus Christ, are good news for those persons who accept what the Scriptures have to say. Even the harsher words of Scripture can be good news inasmuch as they point us in the direction our lives should take instead of the direction we might have been going without God. Yes, the Scriptures judge us and point out to us where we sin against God's will. But they also promise that God forgives our sin when we turn our lives toward doing God's will. When we receive the forgiveness that comes when we turn our lives toward God's love and God's will, the Scriptures are fulfilled in our hearing—and in our lives.

 TOGETHER

(1) As a family, try to remember as much as you can about your separate group experiences during the FaithHome session and talk about them together.

(2) Invite each member of the family to share one thing that he or she heard during the session that was new or important to him or her.

(3) You are now beginning your eighth week of FaithHome. Take the time now to talk as a family about your experience:

- What is the most important thing that has happened to your family during the past week?
- How do you think God was involved with your family during that "most important thing"?
- What difference has FaithHome made in the ways your family thinks about God?

Though these questions are familiar to you, they are intended to help you review what you have been doing and to lift up those things that are of particular help and meaning to the members of your family.

 FAMILY FAITH BREAK

(1) Ask a family member to read aloud Luke 4:14-30.

 BIBLE HELP

In this passage, Jesus had begun his ministry in Galilee, the region in which he grew up. He was probably about thirty years old. His teachings generally had been well received. Now he came to his hometown of Nazareth and was asked to teach in the synagogue during sabbath service there, among the friends and family with whom he had grown into adulthood.

When time came for Jesus to read from the Scripture during the worship service, he read from Isaiah 61:1-2. After concluding the reading, he sat down, which is the posture from which rabbis taught. "Today this scripture has been fulfilled in your hearing," he said (Luke 4:21).

On one level, Jesus might have been saying that the Scripture he had just read had been fulfilled in himself. To some that might have sounded arrogant, although Luke does not indicate that the people who heard Jesus took it that way. Instead, his hearers may have understood him to say something like this: "You godly people are living in godly times!" If that is what they heard, then no wonder "all spoke well of him and were amazed at the gracious words that came from his mouth" (Luke 4:22). But what Jesus had to say next shows that he meant something else entirely.

The reference Jesus made to Elijah and the widow at Zarephath is from 1 Kings 17:1-16. The reference to Elisha and Naaman is from 2 Kings 5:1-14. Both of those stories refer to occasions when non-Israelites received the words and mighty acts of God, while Israelites received but did not hear God's judgment upon them. Jesus was saying in effect that non-Jews were more likely to find the words of Isaiah fulfilled than were the Jews in Jesus' hometown synagogue. These were words that made Jesus' childhood friends and the elders very angry. In fact, they were ready to throw Jesus off a cliff, which was the traditional penalty for blasphemy. The good citizens of Nazareth were ready to hear how Scripture had been fulfilled if it congratulated them for how faithful they had been, but they refused to hear the harder words of judgment Scripture might carry for them.

(2) Read aloud again Luke 4:18-19. Discuss the following:
- What do you think Jesus meant when he read these words and said they had been fulfilled?

- bringing good news to the poor?
- proclaiming release to the captives?
- proclaiming recovery of sight to the blind?
- letting the oppressed go free?
- proclaiming the year of the Lord's favor?

- How might these things be fulfilled all around you today?
- To what extent might your family and your church be under the judgment of this passage of Scripture because these things are not being fulfilled around you today?
- What might your family do to help God fulfill these things?

Prayer:

Close this time with a prayer using your own words or using these words:

Dear God, thank you for fulfilling the words of your Scriptures all around us. Help us to have the ears to hear what you are saying and the eyes to see what you are doing. In Jesus' name we pray. Amen.

Day 2: Living with the Bible: A Daily Habit

 ## TOGETHER

(1) Talk as a family about how often you read the Bible. If you have been following this FaithHome *Family Guide*, you will have been reading the Bible as a family at least once each day. Discuss:

- How often have you found yourselves able and willing to take the time for your daily "Family Faith Break"?
- In what ways have your daily lives changed because you have spent time with FaithHome?
- What have you given up to participate in FaithHome?
- How important do you think daily reading from the Bible has been for your FaithHome experience? for your everyday living?
- What benefits do you believe you have received, as individuals and as a family, from reading the Bible each day?

(2) On a scale of 1 to 10, with 10 being the highest, how high is your family's determination to continue reading the Bible daily once your FaithHome experience is over? If your family's determination is low, what would be necessary to increase it? How can you make that happen? (Your "Family Faith Break" for today will help you to talk about this as a family.)

 ## FAMILY FAITH BREAK

(1) Ask a family member to read aloud Acts 17:10-12.

 ## BIBLE HELP

Paul and Silas had been traveling through Macedonia and had been preaching to Jews living in the important Greek city of Thessalonica. Although many persons were converted to belief in Jesus Christ, other Jews stormed the house where Paul and Silas had been staying and took their host before the authorities, accusing him and some other Christians of sedition against the emperor. Meanwhile, yet other Christians helped Paul and Silas escape in the night to the neighboring city of Beroea.

The Beroean Jews made Paul and Silas much more welcome than had the Thessalonians. Acts 17:10-12 suggests one significant difference between the Beroean Jews and those of Thessalonica. In Beroea, they "examined the scriptures every day to see whether these things were so" (v. 11). Daily reading of the Scriptures had evidently prepared the Jews of Beroea to hear, receive, and believe in the good news about Jesus Christ preached by Paul and Silas.

(2) Talk as a family about whether you will continue to read the Bible daily once the FaithHome experience has concluded. What do family members see as pros and cons in making this decision? List them below:

PROS	CONS

How will your family make a decision about continuing? What is a fair way of making this decision?

(3) If you are interested in pursuing a planned method for reading the Bible every day, consult the bibliography of Recommended Resources (pages 189–191). See the sections marked "Family Devotions," "Books, Bibles, and Devotions for Children," and "Periodicals."

Next week you will talk specifically about continuing the FaithHome experience. Be ready then to make a decision about whether you will continue daily family Bible reading.

Prayer:

Close this time with a prayer using your own words or using these words:

Dear God, help us to think about what reading the Bible every day can mean for our lives, and help us to make a good decision about whether we will continue this important habit. In Jesus' name we pray. Amen.

Day 3: Living with the Bible: More Than Study

Bible study is a lifelong project. You will never study the Bible to the extent that you will know all there is in it or all that it has to teach you. Each time you study a Bible passage that you thought you already knew well, you will find some new dimension of it that you had never considered quite that way before. This is one reason why people who have only recently begun to study the Bible should not feel intimidated by persons who have been studying the Bible for years.

Another reason is that it is not enough merely to study the Bible. Knowing "facts" about the Bible or being able to recall extensive passages of Scripture from memory might seem impressive, but they are not appropriate ends in themselves. You can know a lot about the Bible without it doing you much good! More important is how what you find in the Bible forms you within.

talk TOGETHER

(1) Teach your family one simple method that can help you move beyond simply learning the information given in the Bible toward letting the Bible form you within:

WHAT?—What does the Bible passage say? This step tries to help you understand the information in the Bible passage. It might also draw upon what you can find out about the passage's context—such as from a Bible dictionary, Bible atlas, concordance, or commentary—in order to deepen your understanding of the passage's meaning for those who first heard or read it.

SO WHAT?—Now that you have an idea concerning what the Bible passage means, why is it important? What is the relevance of the Bible passage for you and how you live your life? What difference does this Bible passage make for you? Not every Bible passage will prove to be equally important to everyone at every time and place.

NOW WHAT?—You know what the Bible passage says, and you have an idea about why it might be important for you. Now, what are you going to do with that knowledge? What real changes will you make or what real actions will you take because you have a knowledge of this passage?

(2) Let the youngest or second-youngest member of your family choose a favorite Bible passage. Locate that passage in the Bible. Read it aloud. Then use the three-step method to study this passage. Write your family's findings and thoughts in the space that follows:

BIBLE PASSAGE: _____

WHAT?

SO WHAT?

NOW WHAT?

 FAMILY FAITH BREAK

(1) Ask a family member to read aloud James 1:22-25.

 BIBLE HELP

Traditionally, the writer of the Letter of James has been identified as James, the brother of Jesus. James 2:14-26 shows a possible familiarity with the religious thought of the apostle Paul. Paul taught that we cannot earn our own salvation by trying to observe perfectly the demands of God's law. Even the smallest sin condemns us. Therefore, we are completely dependent upon God's love for us to forgive us and save us from all our sins through the death and resurrection of God's Son, Jesus Christ.

However, the apostle James wanted to make very sure that Christians did not misunderstand Paul. James made the case that while faith is essential for our salvation, faith is not really faith unless it shows itself in good works. Good works by themselves might not save us, but good works are a necessary ingredient of faith.

(2) Use the three-step Bible study method to study James 1:22-25. Write your family's insights below in the space provided:

WHAT?

SO WHAT?

NOW WHAT?

Prayer:

Close this time with a prayer using your own words or using these words:

Dear God, help us not only to hear your word for us but also to do your word. We pray in Jesus' name. Amen.

Day 4:
Living Sacramentally: Recognizing God's Presence Every Day

How can ordinary routines and rituals of family life help us to grow together in faith? What does it mean to live sacramentally each day? These have been the underlying questions throughout the FaithHome experience. As we consider these questions once again, our focus turns toward how *your* family can continue the FaithHome experience and the new habits you have been "practicing" during these weeks.

 BACKGROUND BASICS

In her book *Family, the Forming Center*, Marjorie J. Thompson describes the importance of what you are attempting through the FaithHome experience, which is learning to recognize and celebrate God's presence in your family's daily life together:

> **The more attuned we become to the divine presence, the more every detail of our life together can be lived as a celebration of that presence. Becoming conscious of God's spirit in the ordinary routines of our day and learning to respond take time and practice. That is the significance of particular disciplines like family worship, ritual, and prayer. The practice of sabbath-keeping and genuine recreation is also given us as a means of becoming attuned to the divine presence in life and learning to respond with reverence and joy.**
>
> **Children need to see that the spiritual life is significant to their parents at home as well as at church. . . . Children need to see their parents setting time aside for prayer, worship, reflection, and open discussion about issues of faith: "Without modeling, children may not be inspired to give expression to their own spiritual lives."**[1]

That, Thompson says, is living sacramentally—intentionally exploring ways to claim and celebrate God's presence in our very midst. It is what Brother Lawrence called "practicing the presence of God"—recognizing and celebrating God's presence in our most ordinary moments, such as doing household chores or talking casually at the dinner table. Throughout FaithHome you have been learning how to live sacramentally—how to become a "faith home," where all family members are continually learning and growing together in faith (belief), love, and Christian service. The ordinary routines or "rituals" that you practice every day play a very important role in this process.

The parents of a four-year-old child were reminded of the importance of the ritual of prayer when a sitter neglected to tuck their son in and pray with him before bedtime one evening. They came home to find a very upset child and a harried sitter! They later realized that the simple words of a bedtime prayer not only gave their son comfort and security but also provided a way for him to recognize and "celebrate" God's presence in his life.

The ritual of prayer, particularly family prayer, is essential for faith formation and spiritual growth. Through regular family prayer, children learn the importance of prayer while gaining valuable experience in the practice of prayer. Through prayer we all learn to live sacramentally.

As your weekly FaithHome gatherings are ending, the experience of becoming a "faith home" is only beginning. Sacramental living, grounded in the habit or ritual of prayer, is the key that will enable your family to continue the journey of discovery and growth in faith, love, and Christian service.

 ## TOGETHER

(1) Talk about the events of the previous day. How were family members aware of God's presence at any time during the day? Where did they "see God" in the world around them? In what ways did they see God working in the events of the day or in the lives of others? Give one or more examples to stimulate family members' thoughts.

(2) Look for a "teachable moment" today—an opportunity to talk about the presence and power of God in the world around us, such as when you notice and comment on a budding flower or a bird building a nest or a sapling that has been "planted" as a result of nature's re-creation. Talk about how God's presence and activity are evident in what you see.

Make it a habit to look for "teachable moments" every day. The wisdom of God's plan can be recognized as one season follows another. The beauty of each season can be appreciated as every family member brings to the family table or worship setting "signs and symbols" that surround us: a bird's nest, a lovely pebble, a colorful leaf. The possibilities are endless!

 ## FAMILY FAITH BREAK

(1) Ask a family member to read aloud Psalm 136:1, 4-9, 26.

 ## BIBLE HELP

What is this passage saying? The writer, it seems, is giving thanks to God for God's goodness. In these verses (and in many others that we did not read), the psalmist is awed by the many things God has created in the natural world. We can almost imagine that the psalmist has been struck by the panorama of God's creation, seeing in creation beauty and meaningful pattern. In response, the psalmist sings in thanksgiving for the Lord's good act of Creation. In the verses we did not read, the psalmist continues to praise God for the many great deeds of God that have blessed the lives of God's people. For example, the psalmist remembers that God led the Jews forth from a life of slavery in Egypt. Though they may have been slaves, God remembered the Jews in their "low estate" and led them through the wilderness to freedom. Truly, God's "steadfast love endures forever."

Was the psalmist seeing for the first time what God had created? Or, was the psalmist newly aware of the history of the Jews? Probably not. Like many others of us, the psalmist had been aware of such things for a lifetime. For some reason, however, the writer "sees" those events as if for the first time. He sings—as if for the first time—of the wonder of it all! He testifies to the over-arching love of God for God's people!

Pablo Casals, in his autobiography, described walking to church with his father. He described the stillness of the dark night, broken when they entered a lighted sanctuary and heard the music of the organ. He sang with meaning and power familiar words of the carols, as if for the first time. And he said that when he sang, it was his heart singing. This is the experience of the psalmist whose heart sings with love and awe for God the Creator, Redeemer, and Sustainer.

(2) Read the passage again. Encourage family members who are willing to do so to say aloud the phrase "for his steadfast love endures forever" whenever it comes in the passage. Discuss:

- What do you think the psalmist meant when he wrote "for his steadfast love endures forever"? (Offer an explanation for young children.)
- In what ways have you experienced this kind of love from God? from one another?
- What events in your life might cause you to remember that God's steadfast love endures forever? *(For example, one family recently adopted four siblings from another part of the world. The adopted children were new Christians. When invited to share events in their life that helped them to remember God's love, they responded, "We are now a family. Only God could have brought us together." In yet another family, a child had recently seen the Northern Lights. She responded that only God could "paint the sky so beautifully when everything else was gray during a harsh winter.")*

Prayer:

Close this time with a prayer using your own words or using these words:

Dear God, thank you for loving us so much. Help us to be aware of your great love and to share that love within our family and with others. Amen.

Day 5:
Living Sacramentally:
Family Rituals

Every family has its own special rituals—from regular bedtime rituals to the way they mark special occasions. Regardless of the differences among family rituals, all are equally meaningful. Ritual, after all, helps us to make or find meaning. If you doubt the importance of ritual in your life, try to change the way you celebrate birthdays or holidays in your home!

During the seasons of Advent/Christmas and Lent/Easter, you can make special efforts to celebrate the presence of God through family rituals. In one home the tree is decorated on Christmas Eve. The decorations of a lifetime are hauled from storage in the attic. Every year, the same debates among the same adult siblings occur: "Where do we put the balloon ornament?" "What about this sheep?" When the tree is decorated, the family gathers for food, Christmas music, and fellowship. It is ritual; and it connects this family to all other Christmases, past and present.

Another family recalls the long journey undertaken by Mary and Joseph each time they unpack their Christmas creche. Instead of placing all the characters in the stable, they "hide" Jesus until Christmas Eve. The animals are immediately placed inside the stable, with a manger filled with straw. Mary and Joseph begin in a bedroom far away from the living room, where the creche is displayed. The last to arrive on the scene, the magi, are placed in a furnace/storage room. Each Sunday when the family lights the Advent candles at home, members of the family move the characters a bit closer to the stable in "Bethlehem." This simple ritual is loved by every member of the family and gives continuity to all the Christmases they have celebrated or ever will celebrate together.

Whether it be a holiday or an ordinary day, ritual is a part of what helps to maintain meaning and rhythm in life.

talk TOGETHER

(1) Talk together about your family rituals. In what rituals does your family find meaning? What helps you maintain the rhythm of your family life? Which ones help you to remember the Christian story?

Talk about some of the things that make your family rituals meaningful. Or, talk about the next special occasion or holiday you will share together. Make plans for it now. You may discover some things you did not know about your own family ritual!

 ## TAKE NOTE

Rituals change or need to be changed as the meaning in them wanes. For example, one of the rituals carried out in many families is the bedtime ritual of reading aloud to a young child. How do parents know when the time for this has passed?

A mother has a ritual of sitting on the edge of the bathtub while her preschooler bathes in the evening. It is "their time"—a time of talking about the day's events. The time for ending this particular ritual (and beginning another that can help this mother and son stay in touch with each other) probably will be signaled by the child when he becomes uncomfortable with continuing it.

One family discussed the foods they normally served for a holiday. The discussion revealed that a certain dish, served only on this holiday because it had been served in both parents' homes before their marriage, was not appetizing to anyone! It was quickly discarded.

Recognizing that not every ritual will—or even should—last a lifetime helps you to keep your focus on the need or purpose, rather than on the act itself. Remember: It is *always* a good idea to encourage family members to help choose and "revise" family rituals!

(2) Are there some rituals that you do not find very meaningful or that may require a change sometime in the near future? Talk about them together.

 ## FAMILY FAITH BREAK

(1) Ask a family member to read aloud Matthew 26:17-29. This is the story of the Last Supper.

BIBLE HELP

In this passage, we learn that Jesus wished to celebrate the Passover with his disciples. There was nothing unusual about that. Jesus was a Jew, as were his twelve disciples. And Jews celebrated with one another the festival of Unleavened Bread (Passover) in which they recalled the Exodus of the Jews living and working as slaves in Egypt. In effect, Jesus and his disciples were observing a ritual. It was—and is—a ritual in which the steadfast love of God is recalled. God did not keep the Jews enslaved forever. God called forth Moses to defeat Pharaoh. Then Moses led the Jews through the wilderness in a trek that lasted forty years. Part of the Passover ritual includes eating and drinking special foods. For example, bitter herbs dipped in salt water remind the Jewish people of the tears shed in slavery and the hardships encountered in the desert. Unleavened bread or matzah reminds the Jews that they left Egypt in haste. No time was taken to allow bread to rise. It was baked in a hurry, before Pharaoh could change his mind. Wine is drunk throughout the Passover celebration.

Jesus and his disciples celebrated the ritual of the Passover. However, at the end of this particular Passover, Jesus used the Passover bread and wine to share a new understanding and to begin a new ritual. Recognized now as the sacrament of Holy Communion in the church, Jesus reminded his followers that just as God had rescued them long ago from Egypt, so also the Messiah would rescue them from death itself. The sharing of bread and wine (or grape juice, as many Christians use today) helped Jesus' followers to remember anew the love of God. And a meaningful ritual was changed to reflect a new understanding for the followers of Jesus.

(2) How do you understand this story from Matthew? Does knowing a little about the celebration of Passover help you understand our practice of celebrating Holy Communion? If so, how?

(3) The events in this story happened when Jesus and the disciples gathered over a meal. When Jesus wanted to talk about something important, he often did it by eating with someone. For example, a tax collector named Zacchaeus ate with Jesus and then became a very different human being! Think about meals that have been important to you at home or at church.

- What made them important? Why?
- Were any life changing?

Prayer:

Close this time together by praying. Use your own words or these words:

Dear God, thank you for helping us remember that you have always loved people. When we eat together, pray together, work together, or play together, help us to remember that we are a family that loves one another. Amen.

Day 6: Living Sacramentally: Daily Bread / Daily Prayer

For the Christian, prayer is as essential as daily bread. The ritual of daily prayer enables us to live sacramentally. As we have said, sacramental living, grounded in the habit or ritual of prayer, is the key that will lead to your family's spiritual growth. Nothing is as powerful as regular shared prayer to draw individuals and families together.

 TOGETHER

(1) An old saying states, "The family that prays together, stays together." Discuss:

- To what extent do you think this saying is true?
- Why or why not?

(2) On a scale of 1 to 10, with 10 being the highest, rate the extent that you pray together as a family. What do you think that scaled rating says about the likelihood that your family will stay together? What do family members have to say about trying to pray more often as a family?

 FAMILY FAITH BREAK

(1) Ask a family member to read aloud Matthew 6:9-13.

BIBLE HELP

In Matthew's Gospel, the Lord's Prayer appears as part of the Sermon on the Mount. Jesus prefaced the prayer by urging that his disciples not pray using "empty phrases" and "many words." Then Jesus presented what we now call the Lord's Prayer as a model prayer. A slightly different version of the Lord's Prayer is given in Luke 11:2-4.

The Lord's Prayer is not intended as a magic incantation, in which only those particular words will work. It is, however, offered as an example of the types of things Jesus' followers should pray for or about:

- praising God and acknowledging God's holiness
- praying for the completion of God's will on earth
- asking for daily sustenance
- asking for forgiveness
- remembering that we are to forgive others
- asking not to have to face the things that tempt and weaken faith
- asking to be saved from evil

(2) Throughout the FaithHome experience, your family has been saying and learning the Lord's Prayer. If your children have not yet memorized the Lord's Prayer, continue working with them to do so. Ask your children if there are any words in the prayer they do not understand. Words or phrases that often are not understood by children include

hallowed—holy, sacred, not a part of our everyday experience or usage
trespasses—sins, actions that harm or oppress another person
debts—another word used for "sins"

(3) Perhaps your family has been saying the Lord's Prayer together before or after meals or during your daily "Family Faith Break." Talk about other times and ways you might say the prayer together as a family:

- while holding hands as a family at Sunday morning worship when the congregation prays the Lord's Prayer;
- at bedtime;
- at the beginning of a regular family "meeting" or gathering;
- after a disagreement between family members;
- whenever one of you is sad or discouraged.

Prayer:

Close this time by holding hands and praying together the Lord's Prayer.

Day 7: Living Sacramentally: Pray Without Ceasing

We teach our families to live sacramentally when we teach them to pray without ceasing.

 ## TOGETHER

(1) As a family, name as many things you can think of that a person does constantly —"without ceasing"—for example, breathing.

(2) Talk about how a person can do these things without ceasing. What makes it possible to do them continuously?

 ## FAMILY FAITH BREAK

(1) Ask a family member to read aloud 1 Thessalonians 5:16-18.

 ## BIBLE HELP

As mentioned earlier, Thessalonica was the most important city in the Roman province of Macedonia, now the northern portion of Greece. As such, it was also an important site in which to plant a church. Paul, along with Timothy and Silas, started a church there; but opposition from the Jewish community forced them to move on. While in Corinth, Paul received word through Timothy about what was happening with the new Thessalonian congregation. After that, he wrote his first letter to the Thessalonians. It was probably written around A.D. 51, which would make it the earliest of all the writings contained in the New Testament. Even so, it would have been written at least eighteen years after the death and resurrection of Jesus.

First Thessalonians 5:16-18 appears toward the end of the letter, at the point when Paul almost always urged all sorts of advice upon his readers.

(2) The advice contained in these three verses is easy to read but difficult to accomplish: "Rejoice always, pray without ceasing, give thanks in all circumstances; for this is the will of God in Christ Jesus for you." We do rejoice on occasion. We say prayers on occasion. We even give thanks when we think about it. But how can we do these three things "always," "without ceasing," and "in all circumstances"?

In earlier centuries, some Christians attempted to find ways at least to "pray without ceasing." Monks were persons (mostly men) who sought to focus on one thing only—the glory of God. They tried to turn every moment of their living into prayer. This they attempted in at least three different ways.

One way was to do everything that was a part of their lives to the glory of God. They wanted to turn their lives into a living prayer. For example, if a monk's task was to spend a lifetime copying pages from old manuscripts, he was supposed to do each day's labor to the glory of God. The same was true whether a monk worked in the fields, in the kitchen, in the stables, or anywhere else.

Another way was to observe the "daily offices," as did the Benedictine monks. Different times during the day—early morning, midday, evening, late night, and other times—were set up for the monks to gather for prayers appropriate to that time of day. By observing the hours in this way, if they did not quite "pray without ceasing," they at least spent much of their waking hours in prayer.

Yet another way was through what some persons today call "breath prayers." A short phrase would be said or thought over and over, to the rhythm of the person's breathing. A breath prayer would be practiced until the person could pray it without even having to think about it.

Try learning the following breath prayer with your family members as a way to "pray without ceasing." The first step is becoming comfortable with the words. Memorize them in the phrases that go along with your breathing. Next work on getting a natural and deep rhythm of breathing going. Then add the words, either out loud (which may prove difficult while breathing) or silently:

> *(inhale)* **Lord Jesus Christ,**
> *(exhale)* **Son of God,**
> *(inhale)* **have mercy on me,**
> *(exhale)* **a sinner.**

If you have young children, you might want to use this breath prayer:

(inhale) **Jesus,**
(exhale) **I love you.**

Prayer:

Use your breath prayer as the prayer your family uses to end this time.

 ## FAMILY MEALS

Family Meal #1

- Lots of folks enjoy macaroni and cheese. Here's a new version that you might like to try! (Note: If you have small children who dislike changing the "tried and true," leave the salsa and chips out of a small amount of cheesy macaroni. You'll make everyone happy!)

South-of-the-Border Macaroni Bake

Ingredients:
    1 can condensed cream of chicken soup (26 ounces)
    1 cup milk
    6 cups hot cooked elbow macaroni (about 3 cups dry)
    3 cups shredded cheese (about 12 ounces)
    1 cup salsa
    1 cup coarsely crushed tortilla chips

Directions:

    Combine soup and milk in a large bowl. Stir in cooked macaroni, cheese, and salsa. Spoon into a 3-quart oblong baking dish. Bake at 400 degrees for 20 minutes. Stir. Sprinkle chips over macaroni mixture. Bake 5 minutes more, or until hot and bubbly.[2]

- Serve your macaroni bake with fruit or raw veggies and rolls.

- Light the Christ candle at the beginning of your meal and say a prayer, such as this one:

Dear God, we are reminded that you are always with us each time we gather around this table and this lighted candle. Help us to continue the habits of prayer and Bible study so that we may draw closer to you. Amen.

Conversation Starters:

- Draw upon the "Talk Together" suggestions for this day, or make your daily "Family Faith Break" part of your mealtime together.

- Talk about the day's events and make plans for your next family meal (before scheduling, see Family Meal #2, below), as well as for this week's "Reaching Beyond the Family" activity.

Family Meal #2

- If possible, schedule this family meal for Saturday morning (or Sunday, if it does not conflict with your church schedule). Or, plan to have "breakfast" for dinner one evening!

Easy Brunch Bake

Ingredients:
      1 pound bacon (works well with turkey bacon)
      1 can (20 ounces) sliced, drained apples
      1 tablespoon sugar
      2 cups shredded cheddar cheese (about 8 ounces)
      1 1/2 cups baking mix (such as Bisquick)
      1 1/2 cups milk
      4 eggs or egg substitute equivalent

Directions:

Heat oven to 375 degrees. Grease a rectangular baking dish. Cut each bacon slice into fourths. Cook and stir over medium heat until crisp; drain. Mix apples and sugar; spread in dish. Sprinkle with cheese and bacon. Beat remaining ingredients with wire whisk or hand beater until smooth; pour over bacon. Bake uncovered until knife inserted in center comes out clean, 30-35 minutes. Makes 10 servings.[3]

- Add fruit and juice for a well-rounded meal—morning, noon, or night.

- Light the Christ candle at the beginning of your meal and say a prayer, such as this one:

Dear God, whatever time of day we gather, you are with us, as we are reminded by the light on our table. We are grateful for your love and for your presence with us. Amen.

Conversation Starters:

- Draw upon the "Talk Together" suggestions for this day, or make your daily "Family Faith Break" a part of your mealtime together.

- Whatever time you have your meal, enjoy talking about the day's events—whether they are yet to come or have already come and gone.

- Plan when you will have your next family meal.

 ## REACHING BEYOND THE FAMILY

At the first of this week, you looked closely at Luke 4:18-19 and considered the ways your family might help God fulfill these things:

- bringing good news to the poor
- proclaiming release to the captives
- proclaiming recovery of sight to the blind
- letting the oppressed go free
- proclaiming the year of the Lord's favor

Choose one of the ideas you discussed and put it into action! Feel free to revise or simplify one of your ideas, or choose another idea altogether. Be creative! You might ask your pastor to suggest a specific need of a struggling family in your community that you might be able to meet (bringing good news to the poor); or you might take an elderly shut-in on an excursion—perhaps to your home for a meal (proclaiming release to the captives); or you might volunteer to walk the dogs at an animal shelter (letting the oppressed go free). The possibilities are endless!

If your idea should require more time or planning than you can give this week, take the first step(s) this week and work out a plan for its completion.

Day 1: Living Sacramentally: Humble Service

Each week during FaithHome, your family has taken time to reach beyond yourselves in service to God and others. As your family continues the FaithHome experience on your own in the days and weeks to come, you will find more and more that the desire to serve others is a natural outcome of spiritual growth. Sacramental living involves humble service.

 TOGETHER

(1) You have now had the last of your FaithHome weekly gatherings. As a family, try to remember as much as you can about your separate group experiences during the FaithHome session and talk about them together.

(2) Invite each member of the family to share one thing that he or she heard during the session that was new or important to him or her.

(3) Take time now to review what you have learned during your FaithHome experience and to make plans for the future. FaithHome might be ending, but you will be continuing the journey of spiritual growth as a family. What FaithHome has begun for your family in the way of deepening your relationships and your spiritual lives is what is really important.

Once again, discuss the following questions, considering your overall FaithHome experience:

- What is the most important thing that has happened to your family during the entire FaithHome experience?
- How do you think God was involved with your family during that "most important thing"?
- What difference has FaithHome made in the ways your family thinks about God?
- What difference has FaithHome made in the ways your family lives its life together?

 FAMILY FAITH BREAK

(1) Ask a family member to read aloud John 13:3-15.

 BIBLE HELP

The story of Jesus' last evening meal with his disciples before his arrest and crucifixion as recorded in John's Gospel is different from the accounts in the other three Gospels. Among other differences, John does not describe the Last Supper that gave birth to our sacrament of the Lord's Supper. And John's version of that last evening goes on for chapters with a lengthy farewell speech of Jesus to his disciples, a speech that none of the other Gospels reports.

Another difference is that John tells about how Jesus washed his disciples' feet. This was not a proper activity for a learned rabbi. Footwashing was the task of a slave or servant. That is why Simon Peter initially refused to permit Jesus to wash his feet. Peter was trying to preserve Jesus' proper dignity as their master.

A few Christian groups, such as the Church of the Brethren, understand John 13:14-15 as instituting another sacrament—that of footwashing. Many other congregations observe a ritual of footwashing as part of Maundy Thursday worship services. Maundy Thursday is the Thursday before Easter Sunday and commemorates the Last Supper and Jesus' arrest prior to his execution. The word *Maundy* is from a Latin word meaning "commandment" and refers to the "new commandment" Jesus gave to his disciples according to John 13:34-35: "I give you a new commandment, that you love one another. Just as I have loved you, you also should love one another. By this everyone will know that you are my disciples, if you have love for one another."

(2) Choose the following option that most suits your family:

Option A:

You will need a washbasin, water, wash cloths, and towels in order to wash one another's feet. After reading the Bible passage for today, tell the members of your family that each of you will imitate Jesus' example, as he asked, by washing one another's feet. Let each person take a turn washing someone else's feet and having someone wash his or her feet. Children will be guided mostly by your example. If you treat this time of footwashing as an important, solemn occasion, children will follow your lead, for the most part. If you start giggling, you can be sure they will, too!

Option B:

Footwashing is not as important today as it was during Jesus' time. In the first century, people did much more walking than we do today; and they usually walked on dirt roads wearing open sandals. Feet became quite dirty in the course of a normal day and even dirtier when people walked miles to travel from one town to another.

Talk about the kinds of things we do today that, like footwashing, might serve as a symbol of humble service. One example might be shining someone else's shoes. Then talk as a family about whether you might take on the practice of doing that particular thing for one another as a symbol of serving one another.

Prayer:

Close this time with a prayer using your own words or using these words:

Dear God, help us be willing to serve one another and to follow Jesus' example. In Jesus' name we pray. Amen.

Day 2: Living Sacramentally: Continuing

Today you will prayerfully consider how you will continue the habits you have practiced during your FaithHome experience.

TOGETHER

(1) These weeks of your FaithHome experience have been a time of learning about the Christian faith and establishing or strengthening habits that are intended to nurture all of you—adults and children alike—as you grow together in faith. These habits have included

- taking time just for your family;
- talking together about God and your Christian faith;
- praying together;
- reading the Bible together;
- learning what a Bible passage means and calls you to do;
- having special family meals;
- working on projects that reach out to persons beyond your family.

How many of these habits were new to your family? How many of them were you already practicing together before FaithHome? Which habits have family members enjoyed most? Why? Which habits have been more difficult for family members to practice? Why?

(2) Talk about the definitions of *commitment* and *discipline*. Ask each family member to think of an activity or task that has required him or her to have discipline and commitment. Give an example or two from your own life. (Good examples for young children include learning to walk, ride a tricycle, or dress yourself.) Discuss how being a Christian involves commitment and discipline.

 ## FAMILY FAITH BREAK

(1) Ask a family member to read aloud Colossians 2:6-7.

 ## BIBLE HELP

Colossae was a city in the western part of the Roman province of Asia Minor, a region that is now in the country we call Turkey. A missionary named Epaphras probably founded a Christian congregation there, according to the reference made in Colossians 1:7-8. Bible scholars are uncertain whether the Letter to the Colossians was written by the apostle Paul himself or written later by a follower of Paul.

In either case, the Letter to the Colossians was written in order to combat false teachings about what God had accomplished through Christ and about the relationship between God and those persons who place their faith in Christ. Colossians 2:16-19 lists several of the false teachings current at that time and place.

Colossians 2:6-7 urges the Colossian Christians to continue in the sound faith they had been taught.

(2) Now it is time for your family prayerfully to consider how you can make the habits you have practiced during FaithHome a part of your continuing family life. Refer again to the list of FaithHome habits on page 183 and talk about the benefits you have gained from maintaining these habits. Then talk about which of these habits you will continue. Of course, we strongly suggest and hope that you will continue all of them—if not on a daily basis, at least on a regular basis. The benefits you will reap as individuals and as a family will far outweigh any inconveniences you might encounter.

(3) Tomorrow, Day 3 of this week, will be the last day in your *Family Guide* that provides "Talk Together" and "Family Faith Break" suggestions. In order to begin your own practice of the FaithHome habits your family has decided to continue, make specific plans for Days 4–7 of this week. Write those plans on another sheet of paper or your family calendar and decide now when you will meet on each of those days. (You may want to use this time to invite suggestions and list possibilities, completing your plans at a later time without the children.)

Be sure to make your plans for continuing your FaithHome habits next week—and beyond!

Prayer:

Close this time with a prayer using your own words or using these words:

Dear God, help us to continue to live our lives in Christ Jesus the Lord, rooted and built up in him and established in the faith. Amen.

Day 3: Living Sacramentally: With You Always

As you prepare to continue your journey of faith together as a family, it is reassuring to know that God will be with you always. This promise alone will empower you to become the "faith home" that God is calling you to be!

 TOGETHER

(1) Invite each family member to complete these sentences:

- I'm glad we've been a part of FaithHome because . . .
- What I've liked most about FaithHome is . . .
- I'm excited about continuing _____ because . . .

(2) Invite family members to talk once more about what they have learned during the FaithHome experience. Take this opportunity to share any unanswered questions you may have and to talk about how you may find the answers together.

 FAMILY FAITH BREAK

(1) Ask a family member to read aloud the second half of Matthew 28:20, which is the last sentence of the Gospel of Matthew.

 BIBLE HELP

One of the major themes found throughout the Gospel of Matthew is that in Jesus, God will constantly be present with human beings. In Matthew 1:23, Jesus' earthly father, Joseph, had a dream in which an angel of the Lord quoted Isaiah 7:14 to him. Within that verse, Isaiah talked about a child whose name will be Emmanuel, which is Hebrew for "God is with us." In other words, in Jesus, God will be with us.

In Matthew 18:20, Jesus was in the midst of teaching his disciples about how they should order their lives in relation to one another. In this verse, Jesus promised, "Where two or three are gathered in my name, I am there among them."

Matthew 28:20 contains the resurrected Jesus' last words to his followers before he left them. Again, he promised to be with them—this time forever, "to the end of the age," which means until he returns again at the end of time.

(2) Talk together about these things:

- What difference will Jesus' promise make for you?

- What does it feel like for Jesus to be with you?
- What difference will Jesus' promise make for the way you will live as a family?
- What difference will it make for your growth in faith?

Prayer:

Close this time with a prayer using your own words or using these words:

Dear God, thank you for your promise to be with our family always through Jesus. We pray in Jesus' name. Amen.

 ## FAMILY MEALS

Family Meal #1

- Here's an easy recipe for French toast that you can make ahead and refrigerate for up to 24 hours—a perfect thing for a family breakfast or traditional supper. (The hardest thing about it is finding the pans!)

Oven French Toast

Ingredients:
1/3 cup melted margarine
2/3 cup orange juice
3 tablespoons honey
5 eggs
16 slices French bread, each slice cut to 1-inch thickness

Directions:

Divide margarine between jelly roll pan (15 1/2" x 10 1/2" x 1") and rectangular pan (13" x 9" x 2"). Beat orange juice, honey, and eggs with hand beater or blender until foamy. Dip bread into egg mixture; place in pans. Drizzle any remaining egg mixture over bread. Cover and refrigerate no longer than 24 hours.

Heat oven to 450 degrees. Bake uncovered until bottoms are golden brown, about 10 minutes. Turn. Bake until bottoms are golden brown, about 6-8 minutes longer. Serve with powdered sugar and lemon or syrup if desired. Makes 8 servings.[1]

- Add fresh fruit or salad, depending on when you serve it!

- Light the Christ candle before beginning your meal and say a prayer, such as this one:

Dear God, we're thankful for the opportunity we've had to take part in FaithHome and for the opportunity to eat together as a family. Bless this time we have together. Amen.

Conversation Starters:

- Talk about the family meals you have shared together during your FaithHome experience. What special memories do you have? Which meals have you enjoyed most and why? What ideas do family members have about future family meals you might have?

- Plan when you will have your next family meal, as well as this week's "Reaching Beyond the Family" activity.

Family Meal #2

Whether it is the first outdoor picnic of the season or a picnic around the fireplace in the dead of winter, "picnics" are filled with homemade goodness. Whenever you are participating in the FaithHome experience, a family picnic is the perfect way to celebrate your FaithHome experience!

- What do you enjoy at a picnic? Chicken? Potato salad? Fresh fruit? Brownies? Anything that can be bought at a store or made at home in the summer can be gathered or created at other times of the year as well! If it is too cold to have an outdoor picnic, go to a local grocery store and fill the basket with your picnic favorites— "broasted" chicken and coleslaw can always be found in the deli.

- Assign members of the family to collect drinks, eating utensils, cupcakes, and a picnic blanket. Let everyone get involved!

- If your picnic will be held indoors, choose a favorite family video. Lay a blanket in the living room and enjoy! (Believe it or not, a picnic in the dead of winter can bring on the laughter!) If the weather is perfect for an outdoor picnic, remember to take along fun outdoor games and activities! Whatever the season, fill your picnic basket with love and good food for a memorable FaithHome celebration!

- Wherever your picnic takes place, remember to begin your meal by lighting the Christ candle and saying a prayer, such as this one:

Dear God, you have blessed us during this FaithHome experience. Thank you for all we've learned and shared together. May we always be a "faith home." Amen.

Conversation Starters:

- Let your conversation be about all the fun experiences you have had together during FaithHome. Also talk about how you will continue the experience in the weeks and months to come.

 ## REACHING BEYOND THE FAMILY

You are now ready to begin your own planning as a "faith home"! Talk about how you would like to reach out beyond your family, inviting every family member to make suggestions. Choose one of the ideas for this week, and plan to do the others in the weeks to come!

RECOMMENDED RESOURCES

Prayer/Spiritual Life

Cloyd, Betty Shannon. *Children and Prayer.* Nashville: Upper Room Books, 1997.
This comprehensive guide about how children relate to God provides concepts for teaching children about prayer and includes prayers written by children, prayers parents and caregivers can pray with children, interviews with children, and resources for further study.

Foster, Richard J. *Prayer: Finding the Heart's True Home.* San Francisco: HarperSanFrancisco, 1992.
This sensitive primer on prayer clarifies the prayer process, answers common misconceptions, and shows the way into prayers of contemplation, healing, blessing, forgiveness, and rest.

God's Little Devotional Book on Prayer. Tulsa: Honor Books, 1997.
This book presents the essential principles of developing a profound prayer experience. Each day's reading is accompanied by inspiring Scriptures and the wisdom of men and women who share their keys for effective prayer.

Killinger, John. *Beginning Prayer.* Nashville: Upper Room Books, 1993.
Families who are beginning to pray for and with each other will find this to be a helpful resource. Several specific methods of prayer are included.

Nappa, Mike and Amy. *52 Fun Family Prayer Adventures.* Minneapolis: Augsburg Fortress, 1996.
These fresh prayer activities, which can be used in any family setting, are accompanied by Bible verses and prayer insights and quotes.

Wooden, Keith. *Teaching Children to Pray.* Grand Rapids: Zondervan, 1992.
Written in a practical and anecdotal style, this book helps parents and others teach children how to talk with God in a natural and intimate way.

Family Devotions

Evans, James L. *Bringing God Home: Family Devotions for the Christian Year.* Macon, Georgia: Smyth & Helwys Publishing, Inc., 1995.
This book follows the Christian year with suggested devotions for Monday through Thursday of each week. It includes activities, Scriptures, space for journaling, and ideas for mission and service.

Family Walk Devotional Bible. Grand Rapids: Zondervan, 1996.
This devotional Bible, which uses the New International Version, includes 260 devotions for Mondays through Fridays and 52 fun-filled weekend activities to make the Bible lessons come alive in creative ways designed to strengthen family bonds.

Johnson, Greg. *What Would You Do If . . . ?* Ann Arbor, Michigan: Servant Publications, 1995.
Designed to be used with children ages 6-12, this book contains 101 five-minute devotions to help strengthen Christian values.

Nappa, Mike and Amy. *52 Fun Family Devotions.* Minneapolis: Augsburg Fortress, 1994.
This book provides a year's worth of devotions that the entire family will enjoy.

The One-Year Book of Family Devotions, Vols. 1 & 2. Wheaton, Illinois: Tyndale House, 1988 & 1989.
Each volume provides an entire year's worth of devotions for the entire family.

Books, Bibles, and Devotions for Children

Batchelor, Mary. *My Own Book of Prayers*. Nashville: Abingdon Press, 1996.
This collection of more than 100 prayers, designed to appeal to children ages 5-8, includes familiar favorites as well as fresh contemporary prayers.

Beers, V. Gilbert. *The Early Reader's Bible*. Sisters, Oregon: Gold and Honey Books, 1991.
This colorfully illustrated Bible is designed for beginning readers and includes 64 easy-to-read Bible stories, stimulating questions, and real-life applications.

The Children's Daily Devotional Bible. Nashville: Thomas Nelson, 1996.
This child-friendly devotional Bible uses the Contemporary English Version and is targeted to ages 6-11.

Everyday Prayers for Children. Nashville: Dimensions for Living, 1993.
This pocket-sized collection of prayers is designed to be shared with children of all ages.

Jahsmann, Alan Hart and Martin P. Simon. *Little Visits with God*. St. Louis: Concordia Publishing House, 1957, 1995.
These devotions for children ages 7-10 are designed to nurture faith as they encourage children to learn about God. Each devotion includes a Bible verse, a life-related meditation, questions to help children get involved, suggested Scripture readings for older kids, and a prayer related to the day's theme.

Lindvall, Ella K. *Read-Aloud Bible Stories, Vol. 1-4*. Chicago: Moody Press, 1982-1995.
This four-volume series presents favorite Bible stories in a read-aloud format with accompanying illustrations.

Lucas, Daryl J., ed. *God Is Great*. Wheaton, Illinois: Tyndale House, 1995.
This book is perfect for active, read-to-me children or early readers. It includes Bible passages for every day, questions to talk about, and a prayer for parents and children to say together.

O'Neal, Debbie Trafton. *I Can Pray with Jesus: The Lord's Prayer for Children*. Minneapolis: Augsburg Fortress, 1997.
In familiar words and colorful pictures common to a young child's experience, this book brings to life each part of the Lord's Prayer and assures children of God's love for them. Action prayers, fingerplays, and songs are also included.

O'Neal, Debbie Trafton. *Thank You for This Food: Action Prayers, Songs, and Blessings for Mealtime*. Minneapolis: Augsburg Fortress, 1997.
This delightfully refreshing collection of action prayers, songs, and table graces includes both traditional and contemporary prayers to make giving thanks at mealtimes a joyful experience for the whole family. Full-color illustrations throughout.

Rich, Scharlotte. *I Love My Mommy*. Sisters, Oregon: Questar, 1995.
This beautifully illustrated book shows ethnically diverse families engaged in a variety of family activities while they talk about life, God, and love.

Simon, Mary Manz. *Little Visits Every Day*. St. Louis: Concordia Publishing House, 1988, 1995.
Each of these devotions intended for parents or other adults to share with children includes a Bible verse, a life-related meditation, ways to help children get involved, and a prayer starter or suggestion.

Christian Parenting

Carmichael, Bill. *Seven Habits of a Healthy Home*. Grand Rapids: Tyndale House, 1997.
   This book discusses how to cultivate seven "habits" or characteristics necessary for a home where children can grow in godly virtues and character.

Frydenger, Tom and Adrienne. *The Blended Family*. Grand Rapids: Chosen Books, 1984.
   This book helps parents of blended families break free from the guilt of past marital failure, deal with problems of "extended families" left from previous marriages, overcome sibling rivalries, and build new family traditions.

Krueger, Caryl. *Single with Children*. Nashville: Abingdon Press, 1993.
   This "survival manual" for single parents includes 144 ideas for coping and getting it all done.

Leman, Kevin. *Making Children Mind Without Losing Yours*. Grand Rapids: Revell, 1984.
   This book presents a loving, no-nonsense approach to parenting that teaches parents how they can love their children without loving everything they do.

Smylie, Betsy Dawn Inskeep & John Sheridan. *Christian Parenting*. Nashville: Upper Room Books, 1991.
   Primarily a book of meditations about parenting, this book can be helpful to individuals as they reflect on the sacred nature of parenting.

Stephens, Larry D. *Your Child's Faith*. Grand Rapids: Zondervan, 1996.
   This book shows parents and other caregivers how to build a foundation for their children's faith. It explores the different stages of a growing, vital faith, from infancy to adulthood.

Westerhoff, John H. III. *Bringing Up Children in the Christian Faith*. San Francisco: HarperSanFrancisco, 1984.
   This book is an excellent, in-depth resource for all Christian parents.

Family Outreach

Appling, Mary Ann Ward. *Making Memories: Ideas for Family Missions Involvement*. Birmingham: New Hope Publishers, 1993.
   This book is a compilation of ideas, appropriate for varying ages and settings, for involving families in missions.

Garborg, Rolf. *The Family Blessing*. Dallas: Word Publishing, 1990.
   This is the account of one family's experience of giving and receiving blessings in the ordinary times of life. Whether or not you use the suggestions provided in the book, the concept is worthy to pursue. Hints for families are included.

Periodicals

Pockets Magazine. Nashville: The Upper Room.
   A magazine, written for children ages 6 to 12, that includes stories, prayers, games, and a daily Scripture guide so that children can study the Bible on their own. Published 11 times annually.

DevoZine. Nashville: The Upper Room.
   A magazine for youth that includes daily meditations, Scriptures, and suggestions for living. Published bimonthly.

Alive Now. Nashville: The Upper Room.
   A magazine that is written to strengthen the faith life of groups and individuals and that could be especially appropriate for families with older teens or young adults. Published bimonthly.

ENDNOTES

WEEK 2

1. Caryl Waller Krueger, *Working Parent—Happy Child* (Nashville: Abingdon Press, 1990); pages 103–104.

WEEK 5

1. "Jesu, Jesu," No. 432 of *The United Methodist Hymnal* (Nashville: Copyright © 1989 The United Methodist Publishing House).

2. The prayer "Serving the Poor" by Mother Teresa of Calcutta, No. 446 of *The United Methodist Hymnal* (Nashville: Copyright © 1989 The United Methodist Publishing House).

3. Caryl Waller Krueger, *Working Parent—Happy Child* (Nashville: Abingdon Press, 1990); page 257.

4. Debra Ball-Kilbourne, *Who is Jesus?: 13 Answers That Can Change Your Life* (Nashville: Cokesbury, 1994); pages 55–56.

5. Marjorie J. Thompson, *Family, the Forming Center: A Vision of the Role of Family in Spiritual Formation* (Nashville: Upper Room Books, 1989); page 66.

6. Ibid.

7. Recipe is from *Jell-O Kids Cooking Fun* (Glenview, Illinois: Kraft General Foods, Inc., 1991); page 58.

8. Recipe is from *Jell-O Kids Cooking Fun* (Glenview, Illinois: Kraft General Food, Inc., 1991); pages 16–17.

WEEK 7

1. Recipe is from *Make It Easy With Bisquick* (Minneapolis: General Mills, Inc., 1989); page 45.

WEEK 8

1. Marjorie J. Thompson, *Family, the Forming Center: A Vision of the Role of Family in Spiritual Formation* (Nashville: Upper Room Books, 1989); page 67.

2. Based on a recipe for "Ranchero Macaroni Bake" found in *Campbell's Easy Holiday Cooking for Family and Friends* (Camden, NJ: Publishing Division of Campbell Soup Company, Campbell Place, 1994); page 58.

3. Recipe is from *Make it Easy With Bisquick* (Minneapolis: General Mills, Inc. 1989); page 13.

WEEK 9

1. Recipe is from *Celebrate American Cooking* (Minneapolis: General Mills, Inc., 1989); page 17.